career **courage**

Discover Your Passion, Step Out of Your Comfort Zone, and
Create the Success You Want

Katie C. Kelley

AMACOM AMERICAN MANAGEMENT ASSOCIATION

New York · Atlanta · Brussels · Chicago · Mexico City · San Francisco
Shanghai · Tokyo · Toronto · Washington, D.C.

Bulk discounts available. For details visit: www.amacombooks.org/go/specialsales
Or contact special sales: Phone: 800-250-5308 Email: specialsls@amanet.org
View all the AMACOM titles at: www.amacombooks.org
American Management Association: www.amanet.org

This publication is designed to provide accurate and authoritative information in regard to the subject matter covered. It is sold with the understanding that the publisher is not engaged in rendering legal, accounting, or other professional service. If legal advice or other expert assistance is required, the services of a competent professional person should be sought.

Library of Congress Cataloging-in-Publication Data
Kelley, Katie C., author.
Career courage : discover your passion, step out of your comfort zone, and create the success you want / Katie C. Kelley.
pages cm
Includes bibliographical references and index.
ISBN 978-0-8144-3674-5 (pbk.) -- ISBN 978-0-8144-3675-2 (ebook)
1. Career development. 2. Vocational guidance. 3. Career changes. 4. Job satisfaction.
5. Success in business. I. Title.
HF5381.K435 2016
650.1--dc23   2015028302

About AMA

American Management Association (www.amanet.org) is a world leader in talent development, advancing the skills of individuals to drive business success. Our mission is to support the goals of individuals and organizations through a complete range of products and services, including classroom and virtual seminars, webcasts, webinars, podcasts, conferences, corporate and government solutions, business books and research. AMA's approach to improving performance combines experiential learning—learning through doing—with opportunities for ongoing professional growth at every step of one's career journey.

Printing number
10 9 8 7 6 5 4 3 2 1

To my mentor and father, Patrick D. Curran,
who inspires and elevates my professional life.

And to my agent and friend, Michael Snell,
without whom I could not have written this book.

Contents

Acknowledgments

Writing this book turned into one of the most enriching and arduous communal projects I have ever attempted. I cannot thank that community enough. It began with my father, Patrick D. Curran of King City, California. Dad, thank you for blazing a trail so fearlessly. Kevin and I will continue to carry your torch with us wherever we roam.

The project could not have gone forward without my literary agent, writing coach, and friend, Michael Snell. Michael, I deeply appreciate your patience, good humor, and wisdom as we took this journey from idea to published book.

Below my name on this book's cover should appear the names of hundreds of friends, colleagues, and mentors who have helped and supported me on my journey to a fulfilling career. They taught me everything I know.

My personal and professional network spans from New York City to San Diego. So many people have sponsored and endorsed my work and opened doors that I could never have opened. They include Cindy Tortorici of The Link for Women, Tiffany Bean of Mabel and Zora, Carmen Voillequé of Strategic Arts and Sciences, Valerie Berset Price of Professional Passport, Traci Reandeau of Fuerst Group, Heather Buser of KPMG, Janice Bangs of *AM Northwest*, Emily Leach of Capital Pacific Bank, Janine Fracolini of the Flawless Foundation, the "Colorado Kelleys," my aunt and uncle Gail and Bob O'Leary, Karen Taylor, Emily Kaiser of Boston College, Shana Carroll of Northwestern University, Christina Rasmussen of Second Firsts, Kedma Ough, Melody Biringer of the CRAVE Company, Sabrina Bracco McCarthy of Perseus Books, Christopher Flett of Ghost CEO, Katy Kippen of Grayling Jewelry, Agapi Stassinopoulos, Rick Petry, Steve Weiss of Hurricane Marketing Enterprises, Seni and Bob VanZant, Susan Clark of Heartspark, Lisa Hunefeld of Nike, Christina Cacioppo Bertsch of CCB Educational Consulting, Maria Ramirez Dodson, Maria Gamb of NMS Communication, Arwa Jumkawala, Bruze Hazen of Three Questions Consulting, Katy Mollica of Turner Broadcasting, my Godfather Rob Bond and Leslie Bond, Suzanne Martin and Julie Rollauer of Google, Catherine Marshall of Reebok, John Minardo of Novartis, Jennie Day Burget of Prichard Communications, Jennifer Ruwart of Roger That Agency, Traci Bagli Hooper of The Confidence Project, Theresa Lowe McDonnell, Liz Gaige, Susanne Roberston McComic, Jamie Fornsaglio Hull, John Ragan, Nathalie Molina Niño, Bridget Baker, Stephanie Vaughan Miller, Suzie Sandoval of OrganiZEN, Mindy Lockard of The Gracious Girl, Cari Thomas, Robyn Knox, Michelle Franesconi, Yasmin Nguyen of Vibrance Global, Maggie Palmer of MKP Creative, Saretta Holler Brown, Madeline Roosevelt, and Margot Feves of Opal 28. Thank you, one and all!

My deepest appreciation also goes to the scores of people who granted me interviews for this book. I could not directly cite all of them in the book, but I drew inspiration from each and every one. Their stories helped me craft the book's themes and teaching points. Thank you Kelly Howell, Sandra Reder, Corinne Phipps, Allison Fountain Garrigan, Catherine Marshall, Taryn Edgin, Dr. Debra Hull, Fabiano Cid, Heather Daley, Gerry Reidy, Peggy Leimkuhler, and Naja Hayward. "Thank you" does not come close to expressing my feelings for what every contributor taught me.

My heartfelt gratitude extends to my mother, Joan C. Curran, from Brooklyn, New York, who serves as my bedrock of strength, a sounding board for major decisions, and a source of more coaching than this child deserved. She faithfully proofread every page of my manuscript. I love you, Mom.

Last, but never least, I thank my holy trinity: my husband Tom and my daughters Ashlyn Marie and Abigail Rose, whose tireless cheerleading made this book a reality. Tom, you have served as my informal business partner and my coach every day of this process. Ashlyn and Abigail, you soldiered on while your mother spent long nights and weekends writing this book. Thank you, dear joys of my life.

career**courage**

Beginning the Journey

Ten years ago I reached a pivotal point in my life. At the time I was a driven thirty-year-old professional, living in New York City and working hard to carve out a successful career as a psychotherapist. Yet, I was feeling increasingly dissatisfied with and disconnected from my professional role and saddened by my "party of one" status on the home front.

What had gone wrong? I had faithfully followed my carefully crafted career plan from the age of sixteen, when I first dreamed of running my own private practice in Manhattan. But, here I sat in my tiny studio apartment, one confused young woman with a graduate degree from Smith College on the wall, far from my California hometown, wondering how on earth my once bright-eyed, exuberant self had turned into this sad, lonely, workaholic drudge.

Obviously, the conventional practice of psychotherapy had failed to bring me the joy and fulfillment I imagined it would. After three years working on the locked psychiatric ward of the New York Presbyterian Hospital, I had begun to feel like a disturbed patient myself, locked in a cell and strapped into a designer-tailored straitjacket.

Then one day, while I was reviewing a patient's case with my supervisor during a regularly scheduled mentoring session, I finally figured it out. Sitting in my supervisor's carefully appointed office, I had been describing a particularly harrowing experience my patient had suffered. She reacted to my rather dull recital of symptoms and a possible clinical assessment by stopping me with a virtual slap on the wrist. "Katie, you need to climb into your dark hole and be one with your patient!" Bingo! I did *not* want to crawl down into a black hole; I wanted to climb up to a bright light.

I went home from that session determined to ask myself some really tough questions about my work and my life. After many months of sometimes painful soul-searching, I began to uncover answers that might take me in a much more promising direction. As it turned out, I had actually found my true calling. I did want to help people create better lives for themselves, but I needed to redirect all my talent and training and experience beyond the confining walls of the clinic. It took me several years to get to where I am now, reaping daily joy and fulfillment, not only from my work in "people development" and as a speaker, but also from my home life with my husband and our two cherubic daughters. Is my life perfect? Of course not, but I have traveled light-years from that dark, lonely studio in Manhattan.

The tough questions I asked myself at that low point in my life marked the beginning of a new direction in my career. It also gave birth to this book. I have written *Career Courage* to share the keys to success that I have learned on my journey from overworked, overstressed, driven, unhappy, unfulfilled, and, ultimately, unsuccessful drone to business leader, speaker, and author in love with almost everything I do on the job and in my personal life.

These lessons came from continually refining the answers to the tough questions about motivation, confidence, risk, character, harmony, vision, community, influence, fortune, and life's pivotal moments. Drawing from my own experiences and insights, plus those of over seventy mentors, heroes, and peers from around the globe, I have developed a program that will help you find your own best answers to ten vital questions:

1. What really motivates me?
2. How do I conquer my worst fears?
3. What does it take to think like an entrepreneur?
4. Do I strive to develop strong, lasting relationships?
5. How do I orchestrate a harmonious life while pursuing my best work?
6. What dots must I connect to reach to a deeply fulfilling future?
7. How can I create a powerful network?
8. What steps can I take to master the art of influence?
9. Do I consistently keep an eye on my finances?
10. Am I preparing myself for the next stage in my life and my career?

Each of the ten chapters in this book focuses on one of these keys to success. As you read a chapter, you will explore a topic in depth, developing your own personal insight into that aspect of your career. I know it is courageous work because I have done it myself. That's why I've tried to inject a little fun into it.

Within each chapter, you will find three types of exercises designed to guide you on your unique journey to a great career. "Asking the Tough Questions" will encourage you to reflect on the ways your prior life experience may be holding you back from the success and fulfillment you crave. As you answer these questions about such career-crucial issues as motivation, relationship-building, long-range strategy, persuasion, and money, you will steadily clarify what you need to discover your passion, step out of your comfort zone, and create the success you want. The interactive "Taking Stock" exercises offer playful activities designed to get you thinking even more deeply about the topic at hand. Finally, the concluding "Wrapping Up" segments help you put into practice everything you have learned in the chapter.

In addition, each chapter in the book offers stories about real people (names often disguised to protect coach–client confidentiality) who have tackled the same issues you must resolve before you can achieve your personal definition of success. They encompass an amazing range of professions, from an OB-GYN to an award-winning Hollywood writer to a Wall Street business coach.

You can best accomplish what you see most clearly in yourself. Each chapter will help you to find your true calling by clarifying your past, present, and future selves. Only you can determine what matters most to you and only you can make the decisions and take the actions that best match those values and aspirations.

You will meet others who have done just that, people such as Kenyan entrepreneur Mads Galsgaard and Amazon executive Kelly Jo MacArthur, who shifted from corporate roles to working for themselves and then to forming productive joint ventures with other people and companies. You will also meet Shama Hyder, who, upon earning a master's degree in organizational communication with a master's thesis on the cutting-edge use of social media in 2008, could not land a job with a firm as hoped. She ultimately set up her own digital marketing agency and has since been named to *Inc.* and *Forbes'* 30 under 30 list. Such journeys highlight the need to keep asking yourself the hard questions about what really makes you tick.

Each of us exercises a certain amount of leadership in our lives, because everything we do influences and sets an example for others. Each of this book's chapters will help you strengthen your influence and draw more and more support from your ever-expanding network of friends, family, mentors, colleagues, peers, and coaches. Whatever your work and life situation, you must remain conscious of your leadership responsibilities in all of your important relationships with the people who will accompany you on your journey. You will see how consultant Sara Fritsch used her negotiation prowess to navigate her role and responsibilities when she became a mother and needed to move her family to Europe. You will draw inspiration from NBA referee Joe Crawford, an underperformer in school, who developed such strong professional relationships throughout his career that he eventually took home a referee's highest award for his leadership in the sports world. And you'll gain a lot of insight about the power of adaptation as you watch Doug Fisher go from modern-day Huck Finn with no interest in college to Intel Executive, reporting directly to the president of the corporation. You've heard the sayings: "Luck favors the prepared"; "Do what you love, the money will follow"; and "Money isn't everything, but no money isn't anything." Though overused, these sentiments do express some basic truths about work and life. Each chapter of this book will help you to build your good fortune in both senses of the word, achieving your financial goals and preparing yourself to seize all the opportunities that come your way. You will meet Teri Hull, who went from burned-out shoe marketing superstar to inspired and deeply fulfilled chef and nutritionist. And you'll admire the journey of Singapore Technology Executive Frederic Moraillon, who discovered the value of owning up to your responsibilities to your team. Both aligned their true callings with their core values, made some crucial adaptations and sacrifices, and went on to reap tremendous good fortune.

In the pages ahead, you will find a proven step-by-step program for designing, evolving, and fine-tuning your unique career. I invite you to join me on the first step of your exciting journey toward your own bright light.

chapter one

Motivation: Clarifying What Really Matters to You

Eric began his career as a junior client coordinator at a premier Southern California entertainment agency. Over the years, his natural salesmanship, ease around celebrities, and uncanny ability to close lucrative deals for his clients had propelled him to the higher echelons of the talent business. When a rumor about impending layoffs began drifting through the office, Eric felt confident that the agency would not only keep him on board but even promote him to Senior Vice-President. So why was he lying awake at night, his heart beating with anxiety?

For the first time in his career, Eric had begun thinking long and hard about his future. The constant travel, fifteen-hour days, and high-pressure negotiating had won him a certain amount of fame and fortune, but looking ahead to more of the same made him feel like a hamster on a treadmill. Despite a hefty bank account, he felt bankrupt in terms of personal fulfillment. Fifteen years earlier, he had dreamed of finding a life companion, building a great home life, and discovering pleasures beyond the fast-spinning world of work, work, and more work. When and how had his work and personal life gone off track?

Eric's situation is not uncommon. At some point, perhaps at many points, during our careers, we wonder, "Is this all there is? Am I *really* happy? How did I get so far away from the future I had dreamed about when I got out of school?" If you're like Eric, you must do some deep and honest soul-searching. This chapter will help you gain clarity about what motivates you—what really matters to you in both your work and personal lives. You'll learn that one size does *not* fit all and that real satisfaction comes from finding your own unique sweet spot, the best possible combination of deeply satisfying work and a rich personal life. Remember that, as we stressed in the Introduction, a career and a life are a journey, not a destination. As time passes and you grow and change, your "true north" will evolve. The trick is to do so consciously and wisely.

Understanding Your Basic Motivations

You can begin by thinking of yourself as a leader in charge of your own destiny. All leaders play many roles both inside and outside their offices. Like so many of the women I coach, Suzanne serves in multiple roles as a "Do-It-All Mom and Junior Executive": chauffeur, gourmet cook, wife, mother, head fundraiser at her daughter's Montessori school, and marketing manager for a sleek start-up firm. She feels as if she's living in a whirlwind. And she is one unhappy woman. Eric knows exactly how she feels, although in his case he wishes he could serve in more rather than fewer roles. Both of them have achieved some measure of success, but they have lost sight of the most important role anyone can play: their true selves. How can they recapture their unique, innermost desires, drives, and ambitions? If your race to success has sidelined your true self, you will never find your true calling and your most fulfilling personal life.

Expectations shape us in many ways, but we need to discover and heed our *own* expectations for ourselves and not just struggle to fulfill those of others: friends, family, teachers, coaches, peers, and colleagues. When you more clearly understand yourself, you can begin making decisions that will move you closer to a richer and more rewarding life. Few people I have met know more about doing that than one of my most cherished mentors, Cindy Tortorici.

When I first met Cindy I had recently relocated to Portland, Oregon, from Manhattan and had just launched my coaching business. I knew very few people in town and was feeling very isolated in this far corner of the country. Cindy greeted me with a huge smile and folded me under her incredibly strong wings. As I got to know her, I came to appreciate *her* basic, or core, motivation: to keep people from feeling alone.

Cindy, CEO and founder of The Link for Women, which provides events and programs that assist women in reaching their full potential, has helped countless people, myself included, to understand and apply our underlying drive in our personal and professional lives. To help us do that, she uses Simon Sinek's Golden Circle, a simple diagram that looks like a target with three circles inside (Why, How, What) that helps people discover what really makes them tick. Sinek's Golden Circle almost always transcends a mere job description because it goes beyond *what* we do and *how* we do it to *why* we do it.[1] Like Sinek, I believe it's important that we start with the *Why*.

Understanding and naming my *Why* took more time than I'd like to admit. As I described in the Introduction, I spent the first stage of my career gaining credentials as a psychotherapist but as I practiced my profession I began feeling more and more empty inside. I came to realize that while I really did want to help people lead happier, healthier lives, I was not gaining fulfillment from trying to do that as a psychotherapist. When I stopped and forced myself to reexamine my life and work, I realized that I could remain true to my *Why* even if I radically altered the *What* and *How* of my career.

- My *Why*: To alleviate pain and inspire action.
- My *What*: I work to develop the next generation of business leaders.
- My *How*: I am a teacher and coach; I make use of broadcast and social media; and I have written this book to share my message with a wider audience.

Sinek's Golden Circle helped me to understand that I was not getting enough satisfaction from working as a therapist because I was only fulfilling half of my *Why*. Yes, I was helping my patients alleviate their pain, but I felt deeply frustrated with the fact that traditional psychotherapy felt like such a passive way to help people. Passivity was not in my nature. I wanted to lead, rather than follow, my patients to a better future. During talk therapy, the patient guides the process and direction of the work. This completely suppressed my drive to *move* people toward action. Now, as a business coach, I fulfill my basic *Why,* I just do it in a much more action-oriented way.

Eric thought of himself as a talent manager, but that only described *what* he did for a living. Never having thought deeply about *why* he did that work, he couldn't put his finger on what was keeping him awake at night. Deep inside, below his conscious awareness, he was feeling anxious about the lack of meaning of his life, not about keeping his job. Nor had Do-It-All Suzanne stopped to think about *why* she felt so unhappy as she struggled to maintain the whirlwind.

ASKING THE TOUGH QUESTIONS ABOUT
Your Basic Motivations

Life can get so hard, busy, and all-consuming that we just "go along to get along," losing control of our destiny as we fly through our days on virtual autopilot. So, stop here for a moment to ask yourself these five important questions:

1. **Why do I do what I do?** A lot of people accidentally take a job, become dependent on the income it provides, and just keep going along an almost accidental career path.

2. **If a wizard could grant me one wish about my career, what would I do with it?** I sometimes worry about suggesting that someone consider a major career change in difficult economic times, but it never hurts to dream. In fact, if we forget how to dream, we will never find true happiness in the world.

3. **Why do I care for and support my friends and family the way I do?** It pays to think about the important people in our life, many of whom we often take for granted. Nevertheless, we may need to make some changes in our caregiving, as we will see in later chapters.

4. **What don't I like about my work? My life? My self?** No one wants to dwell on their flaws and shortcomings, but an understanding of the areas in your work and life where you have fallen short of expectations can help you design a self-improvement program for getting better results.

5. **What sort of legacy do I want to leave behind?** Short-term thinking is the assassin of long-term success. People who think of immortality in terms of the contributions they make to their work and family derive the most joy from life.

It may take a while to answer the tough questions, and your answers may change over time, but continue to keep drilling down until you reach your core and can state your *Why* in a few simple words. At the core, your *Why* will go beyond your own personal and financial success to involve those you serve and love. Exercise a little caution, however. You're always walking a tightrope between your own expectations and those of others. Too much selfishness can estrange you from your supporters; too much attention to their needs can cause you to lose sight of your own. Finding the happy medium between the two will empower you to take more control over your life, filling your heart with more joy and fulfillment and, as a huge plus, making everyone around you happier too. That's how you expand your role as a leader. I like the way Cindy Tortorici describes it in her contribution to the book *Evolutionaries: Transformational Leadership: The Missing Link in Your Organizational Chart.*

> When we know ourselves we stand a little taller; we become more confident. We are better able to collaborate, participate, step up and volunteer our strengths, and admit when we don't know something. We are more authentic, and more comfortable with who we are. People are drawn to and will follow that kind of leader.[2]

Taking the time to identify and then live our core motivations results in lifting our life up to its highest potential and brings hope and inspiration to everyone around us.

Designing Your Motivational Game Plan

Your answers to the tough questions sets the stage for an action plan aimed at maintaining your motivations at a high level. A continually high level of motivation depends on gaining some deep insights into what makes you tick. Deep inside each of us there are a few passionate desires that will figure prominently in our quest for greater fulfillment in our life and work. They are what I call our Vital Dreams. To help my clients discover their vital dreams, I walk them through the following simple but revealing exercise (see Figure 1–1).

This diagram illustrates the intersection of the three major components of any vital dream. Success depends on a clear vision of your life's trajectory, a propelling drive to reach your goal, and the inspiration to keep you going when the going gets tough. Let's look at how you can best manage these three components.

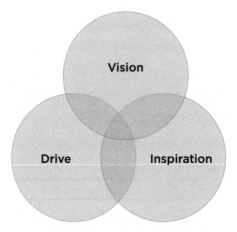

FIGURE 1-1 Vital Dreams Detector

CREATE YOUR VISION

Creating your overarching vision requires imagination. Don't simply think about what you have done in the past or what lies easily within your grasp. Think boldly, outrageously, even off-the-wall. When Eric set aside his fifteen years working as a talent agent, he surprised himself by picturing a new role for himself counseling substance abusers. Whenever he had witnessed or read about someone's life crashing and burning in the wake of alcohol and drug addiction, he wished he could do something to prevent that all-too-common downward spiral. Those feelings sprang, in part, from his experience with family members who had suffered the corrosive effects of addiction.

West Coast career coach Shari Sambursky offers this advice to people who have embarked on a vision quest:

> Signs from the universe are all around you. They may come in
> the form of the promotion you were hoping for that didn't

come through, or doors being closed to opportunity to advance in your current job. While these may seem like grave disappointments, they may, in fact, be the blessing in disguise guiding you toward your purpose. The key is to recognize the signs, the nudges, and act on them. Acknowledging there is a deeper purpose for you and recognizing the excuses you are making around staying where you are is the first step.

When my former client, Teri, set about finding her deeper purpose, she was working in the marketing department of a global footwear manufacturer. All she could see was shoes, shoes, and more shoes in her future. It took her a while to see beyond her current circumstance, but once she got the hang of creating a new vision of herself, she could finally see a clear picture of a new Teri working as a self-employed caterer.

It wasn't so much an "aha!" moment, the decision to trade my glamorous, high-salaried, secure job for hours of working on my feet, the aching back, and the calloused hands that are an everyday part of foodservice. It happened in baby steps. First, it was the burnout. I wasn't doing what I was meant to be doing at that time in my life because I was no longer good at it, no longer loved it, and had no energy for it. My identity had been based on my career in footwear for my entire adult life, but it had become toxic for me. My plan was to make a career change. It was the loved ones who know me best that convinced me it was time to pursue my dream to cook for people. Once I started doing that, the world opened up. I was creative in ways I never dreamt. Of course, success followed, and more dreams took shape. I found myself again. For me, it's always about finding my calling for the stage of life that I'm in. I can't wait for the next one.

Teri went from successful but unsatisfied marketing manager to even more successful and much happier personal chef and holistic health coach. Her vision included two crucial ingredients: delighting people with delicious, nutritious food and helping people live healthier lives through the healing power of wise eating habits.

I loved hearing Teri talking about "baby steps." In my own life, and in the lives of most of my clients, the best and biggest changes do not happen all at once but somewhat gradually as we transition from a tired and worn-out self to a vibrant and vitalized new one. Take that great new vision of your future self and break it into short-term incremental changes or experiments that will add up to the big long-term change you hope to make. Don't worry about getting pulled back by the gravitation of the life you have been living. Your clear vision of the life you want to be living a year from now will keep pulling you steadily forward. When going forward causes you pain, draw on that pain for motivation.

Suzie Sandoval, who calls herself a "soul coach," describes the role pain plays in the visioning process:

So many people are thirsting for their passion and purpose in life but don't believe, make time, or value this innate ability that exists within us all. Most often the path to find this deeply seated passion that fulfills you requires putting on your warrior hat and taking a discerning look at your pains in life because when you connect with your pains, your soul evolves. You learn more about who you are, why you are the way you are, and it provides the opportunity to invite gentleness and compassion into your life.

Suzie went on to say how gentleness and compassion can lead you to teach, share, and connect more intimately with others. In Chapter 4, we'll see how these traits help build the sort of reciprocal relationships you'll need on your path to success.

TAKING STOCK

I urge clients to make their vision tangible. Unless you can *see* it, you can't do much to make it happen. Try creating a vision board. I like to use Pinterest. Whether you do it electronically or on a sheet of paper, fill your vision board with images and words that answer a question my colleague Marsha Shenk poses: "What will delight me six months/a year/two years/five years from now?"

Do you picture more of the same old you? Have you reached the proverbial fork in the road, where you would love to take a different path? Or do you just need to make a few tweaks and adjustments to the one you're currently traveling?

Set aside time for this exercise. Find some place where you feel calm and relaxed. I try to do it whenever I am getting frustrated over a lack of progress in my life or when I feel overwhelmed or stagnant in pursuing my true calling. It allows a little recess from the grind of daily work and worries and helps me refocus my thoughts on the overall direction of my career and life. There's a big takeaway here: periodically updating your vision keeps it fresh and vibrant.

HARNESS YOUR DRIVE

Getting from where you are to where you want to be takes a lot of drive. Have you prepared yourself for all the time and energy you'll need to get you there?

Motivation, determination, and a willingness to give it your all will provide the drive you need. Eric began his move to rehab counseling with a Fort Knox worth of drive, which propelled him to fairly quick success in his new role. He did it on the side for a year as a part-time intern, and then went full time after completing a degree in psychology. A year later, he set up his own practice. At one point, when he needed money to further his education, he took on a few aspiring actors as their manager and agent. Each stage required a steady investment of drive. Throughout this three-year period, his vision never wavered. Oh, and by the way, he not only ended up making almost as much money as he had earned as a talent manager, but in a stroke of good fortune he met his future life partner, Jeff, at a gala fundraiser for families struggling with addiction.

RELY ON YOUR INSPIRATION

Your vision of your best self should inspire your drive. Inspiration springs from your unique set of personal and professional values. If Eric values helping people overcome their addictions, doing that will fuel his drive toward that dream. Back when he first started out as a junior talent agent, the idea of helping struggling actors inspired him, but gradually he found that helping superstars achieve more fame and make more money had lost its luster. The same happened to me when I realized that helping people deal with family dysfunction and psychological illness inspired me less than helping people become extraordinary business leaders. The way you obtain fulfillment may change as much as mine did. That's why you need to keep reviewing your value system and figuring out what matters most to you right now. Remember, this is a life-long journey that can take surprising twists and turns.

When you think about your values, about the ideals that truly inspire you, try to make them tangible and concrete. In her mind's eye, Teri sees Mika, a client suffering from an autoimmune disorder, become healthier and happier after following her advice about eating more wisely. She imagines the delight she delivers when she serves a home-catered dinner to the stressed-out, two-career parents of three rambunctious children. As I work with people like Eric and Teri, we try to create concrete pictures that capture their visions. What images inspire you the most? What imagined situations make your heart sing?

I often think about Gretchen Rubin's observations in her book *The Happiness Project*:

> "Feeling right" is about living the life that's right for you—in occupation, location, marital status, and so on. It's also about virtue: doing your duty, living up to the expectations you set for yourself. For some people, "feeling right" can also include less elevated considerations: achieving a certain job status or material standard of living. . . . "Happiness," wrote Yeats, "is neither virtue nor pleasure nor this thing nor that, but simply growth. We are happy when we are growing."[3]

Sara Fritsch explained to me how her primary values and inspiration of freedom and flexibility have propelled her to success as a senior manager at ACME Business Consulting in Amsterdam. "The #1 value for me right now is to always be in *control* of my personal and professional responsibilities. I know a lot of folks talk about wanting to find part-time or flex jobs, but even those scenarios don't always guarantee that you are going to be reporting to someone who truly trusts and allows you the freedom that gives you that control." Fully aligning with her values put the sweetness in Sara's sweet spot.

TAKING STOCK

Pull out that whiteboard or journal or laptop and scribble down the words that best describe the values that inspire you. Write down serious ones, fun ones, soaring ones, and down-to-earth ones. After you explore all the nooks and crannies in your heart of hearts, narrow your personal "brand" to three simple words. After a lot of soul-searching, some of it grueling, Eric ended up with "service, humility, and gratitude." Teri came up with "authenticity, nurturing, and health." I came up with "truth-seeker, levity, and discovery."

Specific adjectives help make your values concrete and actionable. You cannot picture "Being nice" in your mind's eye, but you can see something more concrete, such as "Sharing expertise."

Scripting Your Unique Career

To this point, we have been exploring the role our basic motivations play in shaping our visions, drives, and inspirations. Now it's time to link those motivations to our careers.

Before you can change direction, you must let your own unique perspective and intuitions guide your hand as you plan your road forward. A few years ago I interviewed Shama Hyder, CEO and founder of Zen Marketing. I chose her because I admired her for accomplishing so many amazing feats in her young life. Imagine my surprise when I learned that she had suffered her share of setbacks.

After completing graduate school and a thesis on social media in 2007, Shama followed her initial plan to work for a major consulting firm but was rejected by them all. She was, it turned out, a few strides ahead of the social media revolution. Frustrated by this turn of events, she chose to strike out on her own, hoping more forward-looking clients would pay for her expertise. Her revised script worked. In two short years, the independent business consulting company she founded became an award-winning full-service Web marketing and digital PR firm with an average growth rate of 450 percent a year since opening its doors.

Shama's story reinforces the need to:

- Understand your unique talent.
- Discover where you can best apply that talent.
- Remain open to applying your talent in ways you had not originally imagined.
- Stay the course, regardless of the setbacks you encounter.

To become the COO of your own career, you must make flexibility your ally, adapting to all the unexpected events and twists and dangers. Flexibility—and grace and agility—are your greatest strengths.

Clarifying Your Vision

Now that you understand your motivation, have refined your vision, and are burning with drive and inspiration, reevaluate your plan using the tools—feedback, opportunities, and gut instincts—shown on the Career Success Circle (see Figure 1–2).

COLLECT FEEDBACK

The tried-and-true business practice of obtaining 360-degree feedback gives you the perspectives of your full circle of influence: boss, employees, colleagues, peers, teammates, close and extended family members (choose discerningly), mentors, etc. If you don't feel comfortable soliciting feedback in your current work setting, then identify former colleagues who know you well, can keep a confidence, and will provide you with accurate

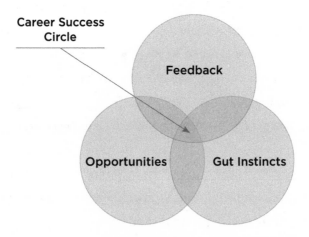

FIGURE 1-2 Career Success Circle

feedback about how others perceived you in a business setting. Tell each of your selected advisors that you want absolute honesty, without all the sugarcoating people often use to minimize discomfort caused by the cold hard truth. If you do this right, the results will amaze you. You will almost always see a fairly wide gap between your perception and theirs.

Leadership consultant Dr. Mary Ann O'Neil describes the benefits of matching your behavior to your values. "As a way of truly knowing and understanding yourself and your behavior, it is important to be clear about your core value set—what values are deep inside you and reflect the essence of *you*. Our behavior tells the true story! Our behavior reflects the very essence of who we are." When it comes to values, show, don't tell.

When I invited Do-It-All Suzanne to get some honest feedback, she finally saw herself the way others saw her. And it threw her for a loop. Prior to this awakening, she had assumed that by trying to do all things for all people in her life she was winning everyone's love and admiration. But she heard her family and friends lovingly but unflinchingly describe her as a hopeless workaholic on the fast track to burnout. "It made me want to laugh, or cry," she said. "Here I was trying to do everything, and really doing nothing to make anyone, especially myself, happy." Could she use this insight reroute toward her next role? Yes, because this aha! moment also synced perfectly with her growing internal sense that her commitment to all the extracurricular activities in her life was not only diluting her ability to give her very best at her day job but also compromising her ability to tend to her own needs and those of her family at home.

TAKING STOCK

Identify a small group of business colleagues, peers, and friends who will honestly answer these three questions:

1. What should I *continue* doing in my career/job? What do I do really well?
2. What should I *stop* doing? What is getting in my way of doing even better work?
3. What should I *start* doing? What am I not yet doing that would further my success?

Much of life comes down to these three options: the insight to continue doing the right things, the courage to stop doing the wrong things, and the resolve to start doing some *new* right things. Posing these questions on a regular basis will help you make better decisions about what works and doesn't work in your life and career.

SEIZE GROWTH OPPORTUNITIES

When Eric decided to move his career in a radically different direction, he tapped his extensive network to gather information that would help him navigate the major shift he hoped to make. Tim, his first mentor, described how he had left the talent management business to join and ultimately lead a global nonprofit organization that supports underserved youth. Tim acknowledged that making the change had taken an almost foolhardy amount of courage and commitment. "It was really scary," he confessed. "I felt like I was stepping out on a very thin limb over a raging river, but once I took the first step, I could not turn back. That limb turned into a lifesaver. I had been drowning in meaningless 'success,' now I was swimming toward a life that mattered to me and those I serve."

Evolving in your life and your career takes more than insight, courage, and resolve. To see and seize hidden opportunities for growth, you should always look to others for help. Your network of friends, family members, coaches, mentors, and peers can prove invaluable to your success.

TAKING STOCK

When doing this activity, keep in mind that you are looking for inspiration. Now, open your mind to all possibilities, perform some imaginative experiments, and search for ideas you can turn into action. Record your answers to these questions:

- *Which of my key relationships will help me move forward?* Who gives me great advice and support? Who might serve as a connector, catalyst, and network builder as I consider a career shift?
- *What new opportunities for growth can my network suggest?* What new experiences will expand my horizons?
- *What can my network provide that will help me prepare for my better future?* Can I find ways in the coming months to test out some of their suggestions?

> The answers to these questions should provide you with a refreshed perspective on how you can better rely on your network in your quest for your true calling.

HEED YOUR GUT INSTINCTS

In our heart of hearts, deep down in our psyches, we know better than anyone else what will make us happy. Unhappy people should always listen to their gut instincts when imagining their next act. If your current work and life situation causes you a lot of anguish, listen to your inner voice.

To cancel out some of the noise, find that quiet place where no one can reach you. Turn off your phone and computer. Switch off the light. Take five deep breaths, hold each one for ten seconds, and then exhale slowly. Picture something simple and beautiful, perhaps a red apple or a bright yellow sunflower. Now replace that image in your mind's eye with the happiest moment of your life. Clutching your high school or college diploma. Accepting your first job offer. The morning your son was born. Finally, think about your future work and family life. Paint mental pictures of yourself feeling the way you felt during your happiest moments.

When Suzanne performed this exercise, her gut told her she should get off the merry-go-round and pare down her responsibilities to what mattered most to *her*—not just what she and her family expected from her. She could only blame herself for having created huge expectations in others, and she had worked herself to a frazzle trying to meet those expectations. Now she realized that all the other people in her life would love her just as much, if not more, if she became a less frazzled and less worn-out version of herself. Now, when she woke up each day, she set three or four specific goals for the day, not the thirty she would have listed last month. If something popped up during the day that was not on that list, she said, "No, sorry, I can't do that." Or she bumped it to tomorrow's list. It took only a couple of weeks for the merry-go-round to slow down to the point where she felt more deeply satisfied than she had in years.

TAKING STOCK

Spend some time during your quiet moments asking your gut a few questions. Although you should make your own list, you might start with these:

- What makes me smile inside?
- What makes my stomach ache?
- What big mistakes have I made by not listening to my gut?

Neuroscientists have discovered that the heart really does play a major role in our lives. What happens to us can "break our heart" or make it "sing with joy." Getting in touch with your heartfelt feelings about your experiences will help your brain make better decisions.

Wrapping Up

Now that you have read this chapter, it's time to put what you've learned into practice. Write a script for the new story of your life and work as you envision it a few years from now. Keep it to 400 words. Be specific. Don't write, "I will be making more money." Instead, write, "I will be making $60,000 after taxes." Don't write, "I will be an accountant." Instead, write, "I will be helping people better manage their finances and taxes." Don't write, "I will be living a happy life with my spouse." Instead, write, "My spouse and I will be enjoying our new home in Santa Fe with our adolescent son and daughter."

Share your new story with the trusted person who can serve as an ongoing sounding board during your investigation into your basic motivations. Get feedback. Revise your story. Fine-tune it. Keep it somewhere handy so you can consult it from time to time. It will change over time, but it will always ground you in what really matters most to you.

We are the sum total of all the stories we write and tell about ourselves. When you consciously draft and revise your work and life stories, you will find fresh motivation to keep striving toward a more satisfying life and career.

chapter two

Confidence: Conquering Your Worst Fears

Cecilia has loved designing celebrations ever since she threw her mother a surprise birthday party at age ten. Now she runs her own business, producing events for some of Miami's richest organizations. She's living a dream-come-true. Or is she? Just beneath the surface of a life full of multicolored balloons, tinsel confetti, and popping champagne corks lurks an insuppressible longing to leave behind a legacy more enduring than a glittering but fading memory of a sensational evening.

But just thinking about what else she might do really scares her. She'd like to write a book about throwing great parties and teach classes on event planning, but she shrinks from stepping outside of her comfortable, behind-the-scenes persona. She wakes up in the middle of the night thinking, "Danger! Danger! Tons of competition! Abject failure! Poverty! Homelessness! Kiddo, you'd better just hunker down and do what you've always done. After all, there's no law against sticking to what you know best." These thoughts have always convinced her to remain fixed in place, fearful to step out into an unknown future.

Cecilia will never do more with her work and life until she conquers her fears. Everyone fears something: the dark, snakes, spiders, clowns, public speaking, or cancer, to name the big ones. But we're talking about the fear of stepping out onto a high wire without a net, the fear that if you take a bold step toward a more fulfilling life and career you'll fall flat on your face, or worse, you'll end up on the street panhandling for quarters.

Where do you find the confidence to make a seemingly small transition from party planner to teacher and public speaker? What inner strength can you tap to make the huge change from dentist to jewelry maker? This chapter will help you take a long, hard look at the fears that might be holding you back from pressing the pedal to the metal on your current path or taking a completely different path altogether.

Our most deep-seated hardwiring warns us that danger lurks behind every change, large or small. How do we override that basic instinct, conquer our fears, and make the changes that will move us toward a more deeply satisfying career and life? First of all, it takes vigilance, keeping an inner eye peeled for any and all stirrings of fear. Second, it requires the single most potent characteristic that propels successful people to their greatest heights: genuine self-confidence.

Why does confidence matter? Because you need a lot of it in order to make the changes that will lead you to a remarkably successful career. With genuine self-confidence, you can do anything; without it, you can do nothing but fall prey to your most desperate fears. If you don't feel self-possessed, self-assured, validated, loved, and worthy of respect and attention at work and at home, your life and work will disappoint you. I love the way Kate Northrup, the author of the book *Money Love*, puts it: "How annoying is it that everything worth having starts as an inside job? Want a love affair that will rock your world? Start by loving yourself. Want your boss to take you seriously as a contender for that incredible promotion? Start by taking yourself seriously." Amen, Sister.

Discovering Your Discomfort Zones

What makes you feel uncomfortable? You need to know your discomfort zones as well as you know the ones that make you feel comfortable. Otherwise, you'll never overcome your fears. Whenever you lose your nerve and find your confidence waning, that usually means that you fear leaving your comfort zone. For me, it often happens when I worry that others will think that I'm not as smart, funny, interesting, compelling, or powerful enough to win their respect or command their attention. Think about the last time you suffered a lack of confidence. What worried you? Did you fear coming across as weak, underprepared, or boring?

Suppose, for example, that you feel extremely nervous about making a presentation to a group of people. In Cecilia's case, the very thought of standing up in front of thirty strangers makes her stomach churn and her palms sweat. She feels supremely confident about her skills as a party planner, but that confidence disappears the instant she imagines herself teaching a class on the subject. "I will make a fool of myself," she worries. "If I stammer and stutter, they'll think I'm a fraud."

From a psychological point of view, Cecilia's fear stems from a fear of exposure, revealing herself as less clever, compelling, and creative than she believes she needs to be in order to succeed on a higher rung of the ladder. We all build inner forts around our fears and nothing scares us more than someone peering over the walls to see our imperfections and vulnerabilities. It's not public speaking that scares Cecilia; it's the thought that other people will view her as less than competent. She stays in her comfort zone not because she lacks the abilities she needs to succeed, but because she does not feel confident in those abilities.

When Cecilia came to me for advice about her transition from planner to writer and teacher, I coached her on ways to listen more carefully to her conscience. The clues to conquering our fears will come most naturally from the sort of honest self-talk most of us prefer to avoid. Not only do we fear exposing our true selves to others, but we would rather not face up to them ourselves. We're all perfectly imperfect, but sometimes we'll go to extreme lengths to mask our imperfections. Rather than let others see a real or imagined flaw, we often overcompensate for it. In Cecilia's case, she has developed a swaggering false bravado whenever she must present her ideas to more than one client at a time.

When she watched a video of herself pitching her idea for an event-planning class to a committee at a nearby community college, Cecilia winced. "Do I really act like that?" she asked, as showoff Cecilia bragged and strutted on the screen. "I was scared to death during that presentation, but I look like a preening, self-satisfied jerk." This insight helped her put her finger on the fact that a lack of genuine self-confidence makes her behave arrogantly in front of groups. What she saw cavorting on the screen was an alarming display of false confidence, which she had created to mask her impostor syndrome. You often see this behavior when someone has succeeded in an endeavor but chalks it up to luck, thinking, "I'm a fraud and do not deserve my success." As a result, the imposter often hides the insecurity behind false bravado. When Cecilia realized she had been doing that, she could finally begin to deal with her *real* fear—that people would figure out that she's not such an expert after all.

Our first step toward conquering our fears, then, is identifying exactly what we need to bolster within ourselves in order for us to feel, think, and behave with more genuine confidence. Of course, this involves asking ourselves the tough questions about our current level of self-confidence.

ASKING THE TOUGH QUESTIONS ABOUT
Your Confidence

Suppose you come to me for career advice. Rather than exploring your background, education, and skills, I will start our session by asking you eight questions designed to gauge your self-confidence. Your answers would lead us to a short list of the areas where some adjustments could get you on track toward greater success and fulfillment. Sit back and ask yourself these questions about your current level of confidence.

1. **Do I consciously attend to my physical and mental well-being?** You need a strong, healthy body to make the necessary changes. Pay attention to your physical and mental health, spiritual needs, nutrition, and exercise routines.

2. **Do I understand how my thoughts and emotions affect me?** Successful people develop and maintain a high degree of self-awareness. Record the thoughts and emotions you experienced during a typical workday and think about what triggered them.

3. **Do I persevere despite setbacks and obstacles?** Every journey encounters roadblocks, detours, bad weather, and even the occasional collision. Seek peace in your specific safe harbors—the activities/practices/people/surroundings that ground you and make you happy.

4. **Do I believe that I deserve to achieve greatness?** A sense of self-worth drives positive actions. Surround yourself with people, environments, and rituals that restore a healthy ego.

5. **Do I feel comfortable expressing my opinions in public?** Everyone presents themselves to others in different settings each and every day. Whether you make formal presentations to large groups or just interact with a handful of teammates, get some coaching or take a class on how to express your opinions to others.

6. **Do I see a world filled with infinite possibilities?** People who have found their true calling don't see life's glass as half-empty or half-full; they see it as overflowing with opportunities. Learn about and practice the art of positive psychology.

7. **Do I eagerly assume new roles and responsibilities?** Flexibility fuels growth. Think about your inclination to cling to the status quo then explore the reasons you consciously or unconsciously erect defenses or build comfort zones that resist change.

8. **Do I take pride in the way I look?** Like it or not, people do judge a book by its cover. Imagine that your "cover" projects your unique brand to the world.

Designing Your Confidence-Building Game Plan

After you have answered the tough questions, you can begin work on an action plan for building more self-confidence. The following three-phase exercise will help you dismantle the walls you have erected to protect your innermost fears from exposure. Once you recognize the real source of your fears, you can begin dealing with them in ways that will boost your genuine self-confidence.

TAKING STOCK

Phase One: Rate Yourself Using a 1–5 scale (1 = Never, 2 = Seldom, 3 = Unsure, 4 = Most of the time, 5 = Always), rate your self-confidence for each of the eight questions above with the number that best summarizes your current state of mind.

Phase Two: Choose Three Areas for Improvement List the three questions with the lowest scores. You will base your initial "Health-of-Self" Action Plan on the specific areas where you see the greatest need for improvement.

Phase Three: Design Your Personal Action Plan You want to specify actions you will take during the next several weeks to boost your ratings in the three areas you have selected for improvement. Keep in mind that change begins with small steps. Avoid overwhelming yourself with that *big* change. A lot of baby steps can add up to major strides. Ask a friend or your coach to monitor your progress.

A good game plan depends not only on spotting areas that require improvement, but also on discovering new areas you have not previously considered. Study your game plan and think hard about any confidence factors you need to fortify.

Fortifying Your Confidence Factors

Since participating in this chapter's Taking Stock exercises, what specific factors in your overall confidence makeup do you need to bolster in order to get on the right track toward your true calling? What, exactly, do you need in order to move closer to the success you seek?

Nothing succeeds like success. That oxymoron makes sense when you think about it. A little success at something, say striking a golf ball down the fairway, emboldens you to do it better, hitting it straighter every time you play. A little confidence breeds a little more, and a little more breeds a lot more. And with greater confidence comes the courage to decide exactly what you need to do to achieve higher levels of success. Cecilia began with baby steps, keeping a journal, joining Toastmasters, and putting a little more adventure in her life, before she began taking longer strides, actually starting to write her book (tentative title: *Great Party!*) and offering a one-day workshop at the local library.

Veteran employment staffing executive Karla Hertzog offers a great example of someone who overcame an intense fear of exposing her weaknesses in a world that prizes vision, creativity, and strategic brilliance:

> I am not a visionary or a creative, but I know a good idea. So I forced myself to join high-profile, national trade groups and sat on big boards. I felt I had to do this in order to continually get exposed to innovation and successful leaders. This was a very painful learning experience for me. I was afraid I didn't bring as much value to the table as others and I realized my opinions were the same or better than the others, so over time I forced myself to speak up and became a better leader and participant.

Karla feared that when it came time for her to hit the ball, she'd dribble it off the tee or hook it into the woods. But she took the club in hand, teed up the ball, and took a swing. No one laughed at her early attempts, and as her confidence grew, so did her skill, until those around her admired her for her clear vision, astounding creativity, and sound strategic thinking. While researching the subject of confidence and asking a lot of people how they developed it, I heard stories about how they figured out exactly what they needed to do and then taught themselves how to do it or found a good mentor who could coach them to do it. In Karla's case, she overcame her deep discomfort of feeling inadequate and invaluable in an executive business setting. She found ways to teach herself the skills she needed to make smart decisions for her company, Innovative Employee Solutions.

LIST WHAT YOU NEED

Some people keep their needs secret, even from themselves, because they don't want to seem weak or inadequate. How do you feel about listing your needs? Do you feel comfortable writing them down and sharing them with a trusted friend, family member, or coach? If not, try detaching a need from some of the emotional baggage it carries. Let's say you have written down "I need to end my friendship with Bobby because he always makes fun of my dream to help other people." The idea of cutting any cord causes pain and fear. Yes, you're making a big change for your own well-being, but it will still make you sad. Just understanding and accepting this fact will help you soldier through the experience.

Sit down with the journal or document you created for the second Taking Stock exercise in Chapter 1 (see page 20). You will keep adding to it as you progress through this book.

TAKING STOCK

Create a list of your five most important needs. Make them concrete and specific. Don't write, "I need more love"; instead, write "I need my spouse/friend to offer more unconditional support when I make a mistake." A list I created while researching and writing this book looked like this:

WHAT I NEED TO SUCCEED

1. Make five more contacts with leaders outside of the United States.
2. Post a YouTube video displaying my approach to career coaching.
3. Book a new speaking engagement every month for the next 18 months.
4. Write 1,000 words a day until I hit 50,000 for a complete manuscript.
5. Find a proofreader who can double-check my complete manuscript.

Notice that I made these five action items by shaping them as a to-do list and that I quantified and scheduled each one. Do that for your list as well. Also, make sure you can realistically achieve your needs in a reasonable amount of time. When Cecilia first filled out her list and showed it to me, it contained such pie-in-the-sky needs: "I need to make a lot more money planning parties so I can pay for my public speaking and acting classes and then I can take some time off to start writing *Great Party!*" With a little coaching, she turned that one vague, all-encompassing need into three more specific and doable items:

1. Generate $7,500 more income from party planning in the next four months.

2. Apply for a $5,000 scholarship at Summerset Community College.

3. Write five pages of my book every other day for the next three months.

ASK FOR WHAT YOU NEED

Now that you've got your list in hand, what do you do next? You ask for what you need.

I have found over the years that friends and family, mentors and coaches, and colleagues and peers usually love it when you ask for help. In some cases, even those who undermine your confidence will agree to mend their ways. For example, imagine a co-worker who responds to your efforts to build your self-confidence with a cynical and even mocking tone. She thinks she's being funny and has no idea that her remarks hurt your feelings. If you give her a little constructive feedback about how her tone makes you feel, she might become more supportive.

Keeping Your Eyes on the Prize

You can't reach the finish line unless you can see it clearly in your mind's eye. As you speed around the track you must make quick and sometimes intuitive decisions that keep you moving forward. Those decisions require confidence.

Intel's Senior Vice President and General Manager of Software and Services Group, Doug Fisher, explained to me how his confidence helps him make good decisions under pressure:

I like the scene in the Tom Cruise NASCAR movie *Days of Thunder*, where he is driving though a fire-filled tunnel. He learns to keep his pedal down and keep driving forward, because eventually the fire will pass and he'll come out the other end a victor. This takes a certain kind of confidence and is relevant for working in the fast-moving technology sector. For me, working in technology, if you wait for all the data to make a decision, you are already too late. My job is hinged upon constantly making critical preemptive decisions based on imperfect data and tolerating seemingly relentless heat and fire along the way.

Doug makes a great point here. Sometimes you just need to stop worrying about whether you've collected all the data you need and painted all the good and bad scenarios you can imagine before you act. You just need to *do it*. Just doing it will build your inventory of confidence. Your goal, that vision of the new you, can keep you motivated even when fire fills the tunnel.

TAKE AN OCCASIONAL TIME-OUT

Someone once said, "Life is one fool thing after another; love is two fool things after each other." Our work and our lives can get so busy and frenetic as we struggle to hold it all together, that we find it hard to see beyond our present circumstance. We all take our eyes off the prize that we want to win in the future at one point or another. That's when we most need a healthy dose of confidence. Confidence helps us pause, relax, collect our thoughts, and focus. When Cecilia acts on her needs list, planning more parties to build her bank account, applying for scholarships, and writing five pages a day, she finds herself so exhausted she wonders why she's driving herself crazy. There's a good reason, of course, but she's lost sight of it in the hustle and bustle of daily life.

When that happens, you need to heed your body's cues, monitoring such reactions as your rapid heartbeat, your sweaty palms, and your quivering voice. These physical responses, as well as more subtle internal clues, such as increasing self-doubt, signal an unhealthy response to stress. That's when you must force yourself to take a break from your efforts to get ahead.

Executive Coach Kim Ann Curtin shared with me some of her experiences coaching women working on one of the most stressful streets in the world: Wall Street. Kim told me that a lot of the women she coaches do not realize how stress undermines their confidence and impedes their drive toward success. To heighten their awareness, Kim asks them to take a break and review step by step the events in their lives that led up to an incident where they felt powerless or let an opportunity slip past them. This review can reveal the confidence killers in their lives. And then, they can begin to confront their discomfort. As Kim explained to me, "By helping clients learn how to live with that discomfort, they eventually build up a tolerance, and they find it gets easier and less unfamiliar over time."

Whether you're male or female, you can easily fall victim to all the threats to our egos that can make us feel unsure of ourselves. I used a similar technique with Cecilia, and her review helped her see that her most demanding client's constant criticism makes her feel inept and insecure in her business at times. I helped her confront those feelings and do something about them.

TAKING STOCK

Follow Kim's advice and review a particular incident that made you question your dream of success. For many, it happens when you receive a rejection of some sort, perhaps from a prospective employer or a person you invite on a date. It often happens during a performance review with a boss or a critique from a client, and it almost always occurs when you receive honest feedback you'd rather not hear or certainly were not expecting to hear. Make a two-column list: Column A for "What I did to contribute to this negative review"; Column B for "Why my critic justifiably offered the criticism." If you look at the list objectively, you will almost always see a kernel of truth in any negative feedback. Grasping that fact can take much of the sting out of the criticism. You're not an abject failure; you are just as prone to making mistakes as any other human being. Get over it. Fix it. Move on!

A kick in the seat of your pants might cause a little pain, but it can also propel you forward. It's all in your head, or rather your heart. When someone criticizes you, you will naturally feel some discomfort. But set that negative emotion aside. Feel grateful instead. You've just learned a valuable lesson that will make you stronger in the future.

Learning to view feedback as a friend rather than an enemy will go a long way toward boosting your self-confidence.

Adjusting Your Emotional Thermostat

Not long ago, Technology Sales Executive Enrica Carroll told me about her tendency to let her emotions get the better of her during her early professional years. She recalled times when she would see coworkers exchange a conspiratorial look or smirk when she grew overly emotional in a meeting. She could have let those reactions turn her into an introverted mouse, afraid to speak up and show any emotion at all. Instead, Enrica schooled herself not to take the disparaging looks so seriously, to calm herself down, and to take a few deep breaths. She resolved to more effectively modulate her tone, words, and body language in future situations. She called this "adjusting her emotional thermostat." As time went by, she learned to advance-script what she thought might turn into stressful interactions with co-workers, her boss, or her clients. These scenarios helped her act and react with a cool head. What a difference it made! Her confidence soared and her reputation changed from someone with an emotional hair trigger to a leader whose feathers never got ruffled.

REDUCE YOUR ANXIETY WITH FAMILIARITY AND PRACTICE

Graphics artist "Trong Na" often found himself struggling whenever he needed to make formal pitches for "Logographic," his small graphic design studio. For some reason, groups of more than three or four made him nervous. That surprised me because I had seen Trong's gregariousness in informal settings. In fact, he seemed quite adept in any social situation. But stand him up in a meeting with a dozen prospective clients and he would suffer a virtual anxiety attack, his hands getting clammy, his face turning red, and his voice trembling uncontrollably. When he realized that this problem was seriously impairing the growth of his business, he asked for my help.

Early in our work together, Trong and I dug into how his early life experiences might relate to his discomfort in business meetings with people he does not know. His family had migrated to the United States from Vietnam, settling in an Oklahoma community with few non-Caucasian residents. His family did not engage with the community or join any social groups or civic organizations. At school, he always felt like an outsider, even when no one treated him any differently than they did the other kids on the playground. This feeling had followed him through high school and college, though over time he learned to shed it as he got to know and form strong friendships with his classmates. Among friends, he felt perfectly comfortable. Among strangers, however, he still felt like a square peg in a world of round holes. That's one reason he had set up his own business after working briefly for a small marketing firm.

What could Trong do to sand off those sharp edges? At the end of this revealing session, I gave him a little homework assignment. As an entrepreneur who had never worked for a big company, he avoided exposing himself to large groups of strangers. "I want you to find two organizations, perhaps the Chamber of Commerce, Toastmasters, or a workshop related to your field," I told him. "When you walk into the room, imagine the people in the room as dear high school friends who look completely different now. Treat them with all the enthusiasm you would show to former pals." A few weeks later, Trong reported that this exercise helped him prepare himself emotionally for a large group presentation to a major new client he desperately wanted to land. "I realized it was all in my head, so I told myself to stop letting my fears get in my way. I walked into the room with the same confidence I felt when I was with my buddies on my advisory council."

You can do the same. Once you have identified what scares you and undermines your confidence, you can set up a lab experiment designed to reduce your anxiety with exposure to the very thing that undermines your self-confidence. My friend Michael told me a story about his father, who was scared to death of snakes. When he was a young boy, his brothers had dropped a dead water moccasin on him while he sat shivering and naked on the bank of the local swimming hole. As an adult, he would rather swerve his car and crash into a boulder than hit a snake slithering across the road. "We figured out a way to cure him," Michael said. "We bought a life-like ceramic rattlesnake poised to strike and set it under the television set in his den. At first that really aggravated him, but after a couple of weeks he would pat its head before he sat down to watch the news." Practice breeds familiarity.

INCREASE YOUR COMFORT LEVEL WITH FLEXIBILITY AND OPTIMISM

Trong's story illustrates two essential attributes of those who behave with genuine confidence: flexibility and optimism. It can take a lot of flexibility (the willingness to try something new that pulls you out of your comfort zone) and optimism (seeing what discomforts you not as a problem to solve but as an opportunity to seize) to get to that self-confident place. One of my mentors, Cindy Tortorici, always reminds me to "be curious, not right." That attitude frees me up to experiment without the fear of failure. So what if I fall flat on my face? I will have learned something from the experience.

Cecelia used optimism and flexibility to make a short list of experiments in confidence-building:

- She found two local women who had written how-to books about their life's calling and invited them to coffee.
- She got permission from a local bookstore owner to set up a display of books related to event planning and offered free advice to shoppers, pretending she was the author of one of the books.
- She asked the local librarian if she could invite a dozen people for a two-hour class on party planning.
- She joined a writer's group where other unpublished authors offered each other feedback and support.

The published authors gave her a lot of good advice, and one of them offered to introduce Cecelia to her literary agent. Sadly, the bookstore idea did not pan out because that setting did not attract her ideal audience. On the plus side, it forced her to think harder about where she could better reach her target market. The library workshop was mildly successful, but with only four people in the audience, it did not really feel like a classroom experience. And finally, the writer's group proved a godsend because Cecilia got candid criticism in a safe environment.

Wrapping Up

Playing around with confidence-building experiments allows you to practice without fear, makes what scares you a familiar friend, and reinforces your flexibility and optimism.

1. Divide a sheet of paper or document page into three columns labeled Best Case, Middle Case, and Worst Case.

2. Write a short paragraph describing an experiment you could do to develop your self-confidence. Cecilia picked the free bookstore consulting gig, writing down the supplies she'd need, and the ways she would promote the event.

3. Now think about actually doing the experiment. Pretend you are writing a script for a five-minute video, starring you. Picture the best possible outcome, a mediocre outcome, and the worst possible outcome. Cecilia imagined a big turnout with a steady stream of customers, a moderate number of twelve or so, and none. As we know, it did not turn into a worst case, but it came pretty darned close.

If you do this activity before you actually complete an exercise like the one I assigned to Trong, you will find yourself well prepared for any eventuality. No matter how well or badly it turns out, you will gain a little more confidence each and every time you issue yourself a confidence challenge.

chapter three

Risk: Thinking Like an Entrepreneur

Joaquin spent the first twenty years of his career crafting public relations and marketing copy for various New York City advertising agencies. His employers and clients admired his ability to convey a product's value to customers with just a few choice words. Despite a tumultuous adolescence, he had matured and worked hard to provide for his wife and two teenage children. To him, risk was a nasty four-letter word.

However, he felt bored cranking out the same old hype. Longing to make more of a difference in the world by starting a PR firm specializing in promotional campaigns for writers and artists, he stepped back and took stock of his life, both at home and on the job. "I can afford to gamble on my future and strike out on my own," he thought. "But what if I lose the bet?" Despite encouragement from his wife and friends, he kept punching the corporate clock, his soul dying just a little bit more each day. "Should I look for another job that matches my dream? I might not find one. Should I start my own firm? I might lose half of my life savings." How does Joaquin free himself from risk aversion? It's not easy, because a lifetime of striving for security at work and at home can make even the slightest risk seem dangerous, and even life threatening.

It's hard to see the full trajectory of your life when you're in the middle of it. You've come this far, and even if you feel short-changed and miserable, you do not want to lose what you've already built.

This chapter will explore risk in different forms, from fool-hardy gambles such as mortgaging your home to start a rock-and-roll band to carefully calculated ones that will surely succeed. It all comes down to raising your Risk Quotient (RQ) and making yourself a smarter risk-taker.

Raising Your Risk Quotient

When it comes to finding your true calling, you need as much RQ as IQ. While teaching about entrepreneurial risk in a University of Portland MBA class, I called on a student from China who had raised his hand and asked, "Are you advocating that we enact un-limited risk-taking in our businesses? If so, that seems irresponsi-ble!" Good question. I explained that, no, I do not urge anyone to take foolhardy risks that usually result in bankruptcy at the career gaming table, but I do champion the sort of calculated risk that can add to your winnings. When I talk about risk, I always em-phasize smart risks. Should you risk your house by remortgaging it to fund that better mousetrap you just designed? Probably not. Should you bet half of your savings account to get off the corporate treadmill for six months in order to pursue your dream to do more with your skills in a new venture? That investment might make sense. It certainly represents a high RQ decision.

For our purposes here, we'll define risk as a willingness to step into uncertain territory in order to discover and expand your possibilities. Like the Chinese symbol for "change" that represents both danger and opportunity, risk entails both the possibility of winning and the chance of losing. It's the fear of loss that freezes us. Those who find their true calling, expand their influence, and build their good fortune, whether they serve as president of a Fortune 500 company or perform in a one-woman rock band, view risk as an opportunity to learn and grow. They take ownership of their own destiny, accepting the fact that each bold move out of a rut can bring both rewards and penalties.

In Chapter 2 we discussed the debilitating effect of fear on your confidence. Here we'll take a look at another potentially paralyzing fear—the fear of loss. Media mogul Arianna Huffington frequently cites a Rumi quote that guides her life and work: "Live life as if everything is rigged in your favor." Brava! If you believe that the game is rigged in your favor, you will make a big bet on your future. You might even push all your chips to the center of the table, going all in. If you think the game is rigged in the house's favor, you'll probably stay out of it altogether. Gamblers with a high RQ know when to get into the game, when to stay in the game, and when to walk away.

The prize of a more rewarding life and career goes to the smart risk-takers who learn to see both sides of risk in every situation. We'll focus on comfort zones a lot in this book. If you don't want to play the game at all and would rather just sit comfortably in the gallery watching the other players win or lose, then you might as well stop here and pick up a book on basket weaving. But if you want to move out of your comfort zone and get into the action, prepare for some setbacks before you hit the jackpot.

PREPARE FOR SETBACKS

Think of any risk in terms of both the short game and the long game. In the short run, you will always run into obstacles and setbacks, but you must not allow them to detour you from your long-term destination. Joaquin commits to his long-term goal of running his own PR firm, serving musicians, writers, and fine artists who need state-of-the art branding and marketing consulting. Unfortunately, he does not attract enough clients in the first year to break even. Having prepared for the possibility that this might happen, he acts quickly when, eleven months into his new venture, he reaches the point where he must dip further into his savings and even takes a part-time position working for a large corporate PR firm. Nine months later, he has built his business sufficiently to return to his own company full time.

Good fortune favors the prepared. Chicagoan Kelly Douglas, CEO of Itzy Ritzy, a children's accessories company, told me how she evolved from working as a high-tech analyst at Accenture in New York City to an entrepreneur:

First, you have to be bold and make opportunities happen, they are not just going to fall in your lap. Second, you have to follow through; you can't just wait for people to always respond to your requests. If someone does not get back to you, follow up again and again, and if still no response, it's time to regroup and assess the next best steps. Finally, you have to really network and form relationships that will get you where you want to go, and sometimes that means working for free.

Yes, there's no law against that, but too much pro bono work can put you in the poorhouse.

KEEP YOUR EYE ON THE BOTTOM LINE

When I began my coaching business in 2009, I focused on helping my entrepreneurial clients raise their RQs. I stressed risk-taking because I had observed that approximately 75 percent of the entrepreneurs I met, including myself, had grown up in homes where one of their parents had started a business or behaved entrepreneurially for someone else's business. The parents passed their entrepreneurial mindset on to their children. Note this crucial point: You can think and act like an entrepreneur wherever you work. Today's corporations value creative thinking and innovation every bit as much as the one-woman band. When I began to shift my client base into the corporate world, that fact became abundantly apparent. My new clients wanted me to help fortify their emerging leaders with the sort of intrapreneurial spirit they needed in order to come up with major breakthroughs on limited budgets. Both entrepreneurs and intrapreneurs need to keep their eyes on the bottom line. That's what Joaquin did, keeping track of his new firm's balance sheet so he could see when he needed to take action and correct for a deficit.

Business is business. To succeed in any business you must yoke your passion to results, which hard-nosed businesspeople measure in terms of profit and loss. "Did I make or lose money? Is my gamble paying off or not?" Don't leave it to your boss or your accountant. Anyone can master the essential rule of profitability: spend little money to pull in big money. The difference equals profit.

However, profits alone do not measure success. As the old saying goes, "It's better to be poor and happy than rich and miserable, but I'll settle for moderately wealthy and moody." Your true calling can supply everything money can and cannot buy. Psychologist Abraham Maslow came up with the hierarchy of human needs: *physiological* (a healthy body), *safety* (a sense of security), *belongingness* (family and community), *love* (emotional well-being), *esteem* (respect), *self-actualization* (success), and *self-transcendence* (a proper perspective on one's position in the universe). Money does not figure into them all, but it does figure. Which brings us to another old saying, "Money isn't everything, but no money isn't anything."

ASKING THE TOUGH QUESTIONS ABOUT
Your RQ

The following eight questions will help you dig into your past and present relationship with risk. Your answers will point to areas where you can work on raising your RQ and, as a result, approach your work and life with a more entrepreneurial mindset.

1. **Did my parents take any major risks in my early life? Did I? How did they turn out?** Some people develop a friendly relationship with risk because the gambles they observed or took as youngsters paid off handsomely. Others avoid risk because earlier ones turned out badly.

2. **What runs through my mind when someone I care about takes a big risk? Do I fear they will fail? Do I envy them?** As with childhood and adolescence experiences, we tend to base our reactions on whether we have seen other people succeed or fail when they gambled on their future.

3. **Which entrepreneurial risk-takers do I admire the most? Can I name friends, family members, colleagues, mentors, or even fictional heroes and heroines whose bold moves inspire me?** The more role models you identify, the more likely you will emulate their behavior.

4. **What emotions do I feel when I think about taking a big risk myself? Does the thought of risking something valuable scare me, or does it make me tingle with excitement?** Careful: too much of either emotion will sabotage your chances of making a successful change.

5. **Can I list my "negotiables" and "non-negotiables"? What can I afford to lose? What must I hang onto at all costs?** Gambling everything seldom, if ever, makes sense. But neither does betting nothing on your better future. On a scale of 1 to 10, you want to get yourself somewhere between 3 and 7.

6. **When I think about the risks I have not taken, do I feel any regrets? Do I wonder what might have happened if I had accepted rather than avoided taking a chance on**

making a major change? Asking, "What if?" about the past can help you create a better future.

7. **Would I take bigger risks if I knew the game was rigged in my favor? Have I always assumed that the game favors the house, and that the odds are always stacked against a successful outcome?** Sensible optimism usually leads to better results than wary pessimism.

8. **Can I identify two great outcomes that might result from taking a greater risk in my life? What rewards would I reap from a successful change in my work or personal life?** The happiest outcomes benefit both your professional and personal life.

Designing Your Risk-Taking Game Plan

Your answers to these tough questions can help you draft a blueprint for a better future. As a first step, you should complete this three-phase exercise. It will help you re-wire your orientation toward risk in ways that will support a more entrepreneurial mindset.

TAKING STOCK

Phase One: Write Down Your Answers to the Eight Tough Questions Put the answers in order of importance, not necessarily the order in which you answered them.

Phase Two: Choose Three for Immediate Action Pick three of your answers. Perhaps you'll want to pick the first three you listed in order of importance, although you may want to include at least one easier one at this point.

Phase Three: Design Your "Think like an Entrepreneur" Action Plan Set aside a block of time in the coming month to put your action plan in motion.

Like a lot of people I've put through this exercise, Joaquin selected the first three questions for his first month's action plan. At the end of the first week, he shared a heartbreaking story with me. When he was a twelve-year-old boy still living in Mexico City with his family, his father, a highly respected architect, decided he could better support his family if he abandoned his solo practice and went to work for one of the city's largest architectural and construction firms. The move proved a disaster, however. The top executives of the firm were accused and finally convicted of engineering a vast corruption scheme involving kickbacks and below-standard building materials. Though Joaquin's father had done nothing wrong, guilt by association ruined his reputation and forced him to take low-paying work. Deep humiliation over his failure to support his family in style caused him to withdraw into a dark depression. He stopped conversing with his wife and children, except to bemoan his stupidity over taking such a terrible risk. Joaquin had not talked about this period of his life since coming to the United States to complete his education and obtain an MBA in marketing. "Making a mistake like that scares me to death," Joaquin finally admitted to me and, more importantly, to himself.

This admission set the stage for some guided research

into people who had won big after taking a huge risk. The list included Coastal Carolina University football coach Joe Moglia, who gave up a lucrative career as CEO of TD Ameritrade to lead the Chanticleers to an unbeaten season, and Apple founder Steve Jobs, who dropped out of college to pursue his dream of building a revolutionary computer. These role models helped Joaquin replace his fear of loss with greater optimism about making the transition from corporate marketer to promoter of emerging artists.

Confronting Your Fear Factors

My friend Harley calls himself "one lucky guy." His wife married him because she loved him, of course, but also because she believed his lucky streak would provide for her and their future children. He told me, "I landed my first job in college textbook publishing because, as luck would have it, the vice-president of a major West Coast publisher was a fellow college alum. When I started my own company, I decided to relocate to Boston because a lot of writers live there. That was one lucky move, it turned out."

When I asked Harley to describe his feelings about these so-called strokes of luck, he smiled and said, "I've made dumb mistakes and failed plenty of times too, but I always *expect* good luck when I bet on my future." There's that word again: *expect*. Do you expect to fail, or do you expect to succeed? The idea of taking a risk can ignite strong emotions, ranging from the terror Joaquin experienced whenever he contemplated taking a chance, to the unbridled joy Harley felt every time he embarked on a new adventure in life. It really *is* in your head. It's a choice you make, not something that falls on you like rain. I love the scene in the movie *One True Thing* in which the main character, a dying mother played by Meryl Streep, scolds her always grim and un-smiling daughter, who has been criticizing her mother's plan to decorate six trees for this, her last Christmas. "Honey, I learned a long time ago that it takes no more energy to be happy than un-happy, so you might as well be happy." Well, the same applies to optimism and pessimism. It takes no more effort to see your glass filling up than draining away.

Accept risk as a reality. You take a risk every time you cross the street. Look both ways, and then expect to reach the other side in one piece. Nothing good in your life and career will just fall into your lap these days; in general, you have to go out and hunt for it with an eager, entrepreneurial mindset. That idea makes you uncomfortable? Get over it!

TAKE THE DIS OUT OF DISCOMFORT

Intellectual Property Strategist at Amazon, Kelly Jo MacArthur, shared her thoughts about getting comfortable with moving out-side your comfort zones. "I want to optimize for choices at every juncture, which means being comfortable taking chances. I al-ways hope that I still am putting myself in scenarios where I have a lot to learn and am willing to take on roles that are outside my comfort zone. I don't mind being underestimated." By that, she means that colleagues and friends may worry that the risk she's taken by moving in a new direction may decrease rather than increase the odds that she will succeed. Kelly loves proving them wrong. How about you? Do you mind people underestimating you?

Sometimes women feel less comfortable than men when it comes to taking risks. My best friend from childhood, award-winning Hollywood writer Gloria Calderón Kellett, writes television comedy for a living. When she and I discussed the scarcity of women writers and directors in Hollywood, she commented,

> You have to fight for yourself, and self-promotion is critical. Speaking for myself, women have to get past taking their work so personally. Men seem to be less sensitive about their work and thus more successful in a lot of ways. For me, I recognize that I am a sensitive person, I do have thin skin, but I think my sensitivity is part of what makes me a good writer. Once I recognized that I was not ever going to be able to thicken my skin, I seriously considered if this was the business for me. I decided it was, and then I decided it's not personal, it's business. That's when things really shifted for the better for me.

All of us, both male and female, can take what happens to us so personally that we fear exposing our vulnerability. We worry that others will see us as weak and unlikely to succeed in a bold new endeavor. Gloria concluded that she could remain sensitive and vulnerable and tough at the same time, what author Birute Regine calls an "Iron Butterfly." In her book by that name, Birute argues that the best leaders, men and women alike, know when to be soft-hearted and when to be hard-nosed. So what if you expose your vulnerability? What's the worst that can happen?

When co-founder and COO of BlogHer, Elisa Camahort Page, was deciding whether to launch her bold new endeavor, risking the possibility of abject failure and even bankruptcy, she considered all of the potential downsides. The worst that could happen? She might find it necessary to give up her home to move in with her mother. She could live with that. Incidentally, SheKnows Media eventually acquired BlogHer, making it the largest media platform for women in the world. Once Elisa moved beyond her fear factors, she could take a calculated risk that paid off big time. If you eliminate the negative as a life-or-death threat and positively envision the big fat delicious fruits of your risky new endeavor, then chances are your own calculated risk will pay off. Think of your big move as an experiment. No one ever made a breakthrough discovery without a lot of mental experimentation.

PAY A VISIT TO THE RISK LAB

Developing your mental risk-taking muscles requires the same tried-and-true process that applies to all of the attributes of the successful entrepreneur: self-awareness, a willingness to improve and change your behavior, experimentation, evaluation, and a commitment to try and try again until you finally succeed. Each of us brings our own unique background and qualities to the process. One size does not fit all. But we all need shoes. Joaquin needed a certain kind of traveling shoes to take him out of his fear of following in his father's footsteps. I needed to replace the sensible shoes of the clinical psychotherapist with a pair of sky-high entrepreneurial heels. The kind you need depends on who you are, what you do, and how you relate to other people, a topic we will explore in the next chapter when we discuss character.

With that in mind, let's move into the risk lab, where you can playfully and creatively mix and match the components of your own unique "entrepreneurial concoction."

TAKING STOCK

Your answers to the questions below will help you identify your unique entrepreneurial ingredients.

1. *List two skills you possess that could benefit you even more if you took a risk and made a major change in your work or life.* Joaquin wrote down "imagination" and "passion for helping improve the lives of others." These skills could help ensure success in the new direction he wanted to take.

2. *List two aspects of your current comfort zone you cannot live without. Do the same for two you could easily jettison.* Joaquin's non-negotiables were "food on the table for my family" and "my health." He promised himself to keep building his rainy day fund and not to work himself into a nervous wreck. His negotiables were "a fancy office" and "a new car." He'd work out of his garage and keep driving his battered old Subaru.

3. *Imagine the worst-case and best-case scenarios for your desired move.* Joaquin figured that if the worst happened and he failed miserably, he could always go back to the world of corporate marketing. In the best case, he would finally take joy from seeing his dream come true.

This experiment can provide the swift kick in the pants you need to go from dreamer to doer, from fearful mouse afraid of taking a risk to an entrepreneurial lion willing to bet on a better future.

Sometimes, however, that kick in the pants can come from other people. For Kelly Kline, Economic Development Director for Fremont, California, it came from a 360-degree feedback experience at work. She had always thought of herself as a comfort-zone sort of person, but it turned out that her coworkers saw her as a highly courageous agent for change (that is, as a risk-taking entrepreneur). The feedback encouraged taking an even more creative and imaginative approach to the work she and her people do. "This is something we need to do more of—working to create this kind of thinking environment, since we all know we can't continue to do things the old way, no matter what industry we call home." The feedback encouraged her to amplify her natural risk-taking abilities and reposition them as a huge asset for her team and her organization.

Remembering Your Passion Purpose

During follow-up sessions, my clients often admit that after learning to raise their RQ, they suffered a setback when the old fear of loss came back with a vengeance. Joaquin had been making steady progress with his new not-for-profit marketing work, when a major client ran into financial trouble and had to cancel a half-million-dollar campaign. "I made a big mistake. I'd better give up this stupid dream before it bankrupts me," Joaquin told himself. That's when I remind the client to remember the passion that drove them in a new direction. You lose one big bet. Don't let it drive you out of the game. Keep your eye on your goal and keep on playing. Remind yourself of the Why you defined in Chapter 1.

Poker players sometimes "double down," meaning they follow up a bad hand with even more aggressive play. When you suffer that inevitable setback on your new path, don't run away and hide, get more aggressive. Doug Fisher, Corporate Vice President and General Manager of Software and Services Group at Intel, described how he does that:

> One of my favorite quotes is from Michael Lewis's *Liars Poker*, where he talks about a person waking up each morning "ready to bite the ass off a bear." If I don't feel this way, then I've probably lost my edge. I also believe it's important to continually be stretched. If I don't feel at some point every day, "What the hell is going on here?" then I know I am likely not pushing myself enough. When I get to a point where I know what's in store each day and that I can get it right before I even start, then I know it's time to make a move because I'm not pushing my boundaries enough and challenging the status quo.

That's an aggressive entrepreneur talking. When push comes to shove, the pushy shove harder.

Perfecting Your Entrepreneurial Trifecta

Born in Copenhagen in 1974, Mads Galsgaard has lived a life filled with entrepreneurial risk-taking. I often cite him as the prime example of someone relying on raw entrepreneurial prowess to drive ever closer to an ultimate dream. At age fifteen he began a fireworks business, and at seventeen he started importing computer accessories. School bored him; starting and running businesses fascinated him. Despite poor grades in school, he eventually attended Willamette University, where he co-founded NetPoint, which by 1998 had grown into Europe's biggest IT Education Centre. After graduating with a degree in Innovation and Entrepreneurship, Mads went on to manage world-class football (soccer) stars in Barcelona, Spain, for three years. Then he became a partner in a small Danish mobile technology company (Inmobia), which serves emerging markets. That took him to Kenya, where he now works and lives. When I asked him about his life's journey, he said,

> Katie, I have learned (almost) nothing from hitting the home runs, except for being in the right place at the right time, which is instinct, luck, or hard work, often in combination. The true dilemma for innovative people is that a product that ends up taking a market by storm has often been launched before without success. Skype is a good example. Other companies (Net2Phone, for instance) launched similar products way earlier, but they never reached critical mass due to the old dial-up Internet access in homes at the time. When Skype launched, people had gotten broadband (DSL), and suddenly bandwidth was no longer an issue. Timing is the alpha and omega: having the right product, at the right time, in front of the right audience.

Memorize those three elements of entrepreneurial success:

1. **The right product:** your skills and experience.

2. **The right time:** now or possibly six months or a year from now.

3. **The right audience:** new employer, different industry, different target market.

I call this the entrepreneurial trifecta.

TAKING STOCK

Flesh out your own entrepreneurial trifecta.

1. *What is your perfect product?* Think in terms of the skills and experience you can transfer to a new job or a new endeavor.

2. *When should you make your move?* Draw up an aggressive schedule, promising to make a bet by a specific date.

3. *What audience should you tackle?* Name potential employers who could provide you with your dream job. If you want to start your own business, give it a name.

Joaquin's trifecta looked like this:

1. "I know a lot about branding and marketing that applies to all types of organizations, including novelists, singers, and sculptors."

2. "I will start my new consulting company the day my savings account reaches $50,000, enough to support

me and my family for almost a year, even if my busi-ness has not broken even by that point."

3. "I will serve artists in all fields, and I will call my new business ArtBrand International."

Dreams live in your head. They are like smoke without a fire. They will never get hot unless you take them from the world of abstract thinking and flesh them out with specific, concrete words and actions.

Wrapping Up

Clare McGrory, who serves as the Vice President of Finance and Retail Marketing at Sunoco, taught me how to raise my RQ and think like an entrepreneur by playing a little game with myself.

The way I have gained confidence and built momen-tum is by putting myself at risk in situations where I am vulnerable and at risk of failure. This has been the crit-ical component for me to make actual step changes in my career. Have I risked failure? Often! But you can't get anywhere without putting yourself in new situa-tions. I start out small:

I invite myself to meetings where I think *I can learn* something that will help me do my job better, even if it's not directly related to my work.

I also invite myself to meetings that I think *can benefit from my input.*

And I invite myself to meetings where I think *my voice should be heard.* Nine times out of ten, nobody objects.

From there I build momentum in my career—both in my own knowledge and experience—and in how I am perceived."

I love Clare's idea of "risk by invitation." On a sheet of paper, write down what invitations you should issue yourself. Which "parties" will put you in a risky place and let you flex your entrepreneurial muscles? As Clare does, make sure you include all three opportunities to learn and grow:

1. Risk Party #1: Where I can learn something that will contribute to my career evolution.
2. Risk Party #2: Where I can share something that will benefit other people's careers.
3. Risk Party #3: Where I can make my voice heard.

It's important to think of these opportunities as something fun to do, not as dreaded homework assignments. Experiment, play, and enjoy yourself and the people you meet. There's no better way to take the fear of loss out of your entrepreneurial mindset.

chapter four

Character: Linking Who You Are and What You Do to How You Relate to People

Matma, a highly skilled IT professional working in London, England, consistently wins praise for her laserlike analytical skills. She can fix even the most pesky glitches that befuddle the rest of the systems team. Taking great pride in her perfectionism, she loves to impress her nontechnical colleagues with her wizardry. She expects a major promotion during her upcoming performance review.

Imagine her devastation when her boss, Bob, gives her low marks for her interpersonal skills, something she must master before she can move up the corporate ladder. "What do you mean by interpersonal skills?" she asks. "I get along very well with everybody."

Bob sighs. "You do brilliant work, yes, but your teammates don't fully trust you to look out for everyone's welfare. Some even sense you might leave for a better job any day. The folks in other departments figure you're hiding something behind all your technical jargon."

If Matma were to ask my opinion, I'd tell her she needs to lighten up, and feel confident about her technical skills, but spend a lot of time cultivating more personal power by learning to communicate more effectively with her colleagues and everyone else she works with. She needs to replace her image as Smartest Geek in the Room to Technical Wizard Most Likely to Succeed as a Manager. The first three chapters explored three essential ingredients for a successful career: motivation, confidence, and the ability to take risks. This chapter will focus on a more elusive trait: character.

We define character as the manner in which others perceive you. It represents a combination of who you are, what you do, and how you relate to people. In contrast, when we refer to someone's personality, this typically encompasses their sensibilities and mannerisms on more of a subjective level. A sterling character draws the admiration of others and makes them want to work with you. Matma has nailed the first two. She's an exceptionally intelligent woman. She performs technical magic. But when it comes to relating to people, she couldn't find a clue with an electron microscope. I would argue that her character lacks a crucial dimension. She is not tuned into the nuances of her working relationships and the tremendous value that this arena has when pursuing management growth.

If she doesn't fix it, she'll never win a management position.

And if her manager *does* happen to promote her, she won't last long if her people do not admire her and enjoy working with her. How can she set about building the sort of meaningful and effective working relationships she needs to win a reputation as an excellent management candidate with the character she needs to succeed in the position?

She can start by paying closer attention to how she links who she is and what she does with how she relates to people. The right linkage creates dynamic and rich working relationships. Such relationships thrive on trust, transparency, and loyalty. When people trust you, when they know you will always tell them the truth, and when they know they can depend on you through thick and thin, they will jump at the chance to play with you.

Playing Well with Others

You may know the Girl Scout law: "I will do my best to be honest and fair, friendly and helpful, considerate and caring, courageous and strong, and responsible for what I say and do, and to respect myself and others, respect authority, use resources wisely, make the world a better place, and be a sister to every Girl Scout." Of course, that applies to males as well. This commitment might seem old-fashioned to some people in our increasingly cynical world, but many people believe that a person's character depends on such traits. Isn't that what Matma wants, for people to perceive her as a "good scout"?

When it comes to building character, I have picked out three traits that I think, more than any others, make you a good scout in the eyes of coworkers, friends, and family.

BE TRUSTWORTHY

There's a joke about putting your hand on your wallet when someone says, "Trust me." You can't ask for trust, you can only prove yourself trustworthy. No solid and productive relationship can exist without it. With it, collaboration, creative problem solving, and achievement flourish. In Chapter 3, we emphasized the need for developing a high Risk Quotient (RQ). Trust requires a high Emotional Quotient (EQ). Author Daniel Goleman coined the phrase Emotional Intelligence (EI) to encompass a wide array of competencies and skills that drive success at work and in life. According to Goleman, EI consists of five key components of emotional intelligence: motivation, self-awareness, self-regulation, social skill, and empathy.[1] In Chapter 1, we dug deeply into your motivation, in Chapter 2 we tackled self-awareness and self-regulation, which we called self-modulation. Now we'll turn our attention to social skill and empathy.

Here's where Matma should pay close attention. Her lack of sufficient social skill and empathy has caused her coworkers to view her as a flight risk and someone more concerned with her own success than that of the team. If she possessed more empathy and social skill she might see that her technical lingo intimidates nontechnical peers and raises doubts about her reliability as a team player. She would see that she has been erecting fences where she should have been opening doors and constructing bridges.

Lieutenant Colonel (Ret.) Pete Rooks, Director of Leadership at the University of Portland, spent over twenty-one years in the military and observed that, "Leaders need to have strong emotional intelligence: they must be able to earn respect and build trust, create and facilitate culture, be people of their word, and elevate others, along the lines of a 'I don't care how much you know until I know how much you care' kind of mentality."

Care. If people believe that you care for them, they will care for you, in more ways than one. Matma would gain a lot of support for her promotion if everyone around her, especially her boss, knew in their hearts that she cares about others as much as she cares about herself.

TAKING STOCK

While success does not depend on your winning a popularity contest, your ability to attract and hold people to your sphere of influence does. Spend some time carefully rating yourself with respect to the following characteristics of strong workplace relationships. Do you display that characteristic Always, Usually, Sometimes, or Seldom? I left out "Never" because, in that case, you need more than a book to teach you how to get along with others (just kidding). You might also ask a mentor or trusted coworker to give you some feedback on your relationship-building skills.

- *I feel confident about my interactions with others at work.* Do any of your colleagues make you feel uncomfortable? Do others freely open up to you on a personal level, or do they tend to avoid engaging in conversations about anything that does not pertain to work? Matma comes to see that her inherent shyness keeps her at arm's length from her teammates and others in the company. To protect her sense of vulnerability, she maintains a hard exterior shell and uses highfalutin jargon to maintain a distance between herself and her colleagues. This insight prompts her to ask more questions about her workmates' lives outside the office and to offer them some stories of her childhood in Calcutta.

- *I deeply care about the people at work.* Can you put yourself in the shoes of a colleague who has been going through some troubling personal or professional issues? Have you developed relationships with people with whom you can share your own concerns? As Matma relaxes her guard and learns more about her teammates on a personal level, she finds them much more open in her presence. To her amazement, people love her funny anecdotes about life in India. Telling these stories, she reveals a dry sense of humor that makes her colleagues laugh out loud.

- *I readily admit that I need help with a problem.* When you express a need for support, do others rush to your rescue? It doesn't take a psychotherapist to tell Matma that she has avoided asking for help because that would reveal the fact that she does not know everything about everything. While she finds it hard to start admitting mistakes or gaps in her knowledge, she takes heart from the fact that the first time she tells her teammates about a problem that has been baffling her she receives a warm reception, not the disapproval she had feared.

- *I do what I say I will do.* If you cannot deliver as expected, do you quickly explain the reason for the setback? Matma has built a reputation for getting the job done well and on time. People trust her to do her work. However, that trust does not extend to the personal level, where they suspect she worries more about her own advancement than the welfare of the team. This realization leads Matma to put herself on a less aggressive timetable for promotion. Paradoxically, this puts her on a faster track when her boss sees how well she has been relating to her peers

- *I provide encouragement to my coworkers.* Can you act as the cheerleader when the team needs an emotional boost? Matma cannot see herself performing jumping jacks and waving pompoms to add to the positive environment at work, but she can certainly offer sincere encouragement to her fellow workers and put more effort into congratulating someone on a job well done. She gets a chuckle from Bob when she offers him a high five after he solves a nettlesome problem with a bug in the software.

Fruitful and dynamic relationships thrive in an environment where people trust one another. Anyone can learn to be a more trustworthy person by simply looking more carefully at the social dynamics taking place in their work environment.

BE TRANSPARENT

I use the word "transparency" to mean "honesty on steroids." When I teach a class about the importance of trust, I often refer to the Johari Window, a framework created in 1955 by two American psychologists, Joseph Luft and Harrington Ingham. It can help you better understand yourself and your relationship

with others. Take a look at Figure 4–1, before completing the
next exercise:

JOHARI WINDOW

	Known to Self	Not Known to Self
Known to Others	Arena	Blind Spot
Not Known to Others	Facade	Unknown

TAKING STOCK

Pick five or six adjectives that best describe your own personality. Matma lists "self-sufficient, serious, reserved, calm, and ambitious." Now ask someone you trust, a coworker, friend, or family member, to come up with five adjectives they think best describe your personality. Matma's best friend Freda writes down "professional, shy, mysterious, lonely, and ambitious." Now you can place the ten adjectives in the appropriate panels of the Johari Window.

Matma and Freda decide that "shy and reserved" and "serious and professional" describe more or less the same traits.

So they put those words in the Arena panel (qualities known to both self and others). Since Freda's list does not include "self-sufficient" or "calm," they place those words in the Facade panel (false fronts or masks Matma hides behind). That leaves Freda's last two descriptors, "mysterious" and "lonely," which they place in the Blind Spot panel (traits Matma doesn't see in herself, but others can). What about the Unknown panel? Together, they ponder adjectives neither of them listed that other people might use to describe Matma's personality. After some playful discussion, they come up with "scary."

You can see that someone will want to work on the traits in their Facade and Blind Spot panels. Just acknowledging them puts you on a path toward self-improvement in areas that will enhance your relationships with others. You clean the Window, you become more transparent. Bottom line: Greater self-awareness sustains more dynamic relationships, which, in turn, propel you toward greater success at work and in life.

Christopher Flett, founder and CEO of Ghost CEO, has worked with 25,000 professional women who wish to enhance their leadership skills. He told me, "A key issue for women is that they do not understand that they are the authors of their reputation. Men typically will craft their reputation to their desiring and then sell it as fact. Women tend to let the world determine their reputation and just go along with this sometimes underrepresented and vastly underestimated bill of goods." What does this mean to Matma? With her Facade and Blind Spot lists in mind, she can take charge of improving the way others perceive her and thus the way she and they relate to one another. The transparent Matma will always win out over the Matma who does not base her relationships on absolute honesty.

BE LOYAL

Let's assume you enjoy relationships based on trust and honesty. Is that all you need? No, you need one more essential ingredient: loyalty. You need people who will stand up for you, no matter what; who will stay by your side when the going gets rough; who you can always count on to "have your back."

An investment in loyalty can pay off big time. I love the story that Deepak Chopra, the renowned spiritual guide, tells about his father, Krishnan. During World War II, the elder Chopra, who had earned a medical degree in 1943, served as a medic at Kohima, one of the bloodiest battles with the Japanese on the subcontinent. Britain had controlled India for more than a century and treated the native population as little more than slaves. However, due to his medical expertise, Krishnan had earned the rank of lieutenant, a rare accomplishment for an Indian soldier. After the war, Lord Mountbatten, the British Viceroy of India, rewarded Krishnan for his loyal service with a scholarship to attend medical school in England, where the young doctor studied to become a cardiologist. His loyalty to the British paid off big time and set the stage for his son Deepak to become a household name in the field of human development.

Now, I'm not suggesting you remain loyal to a toxic boss. As we discussed in the previous chapter, you need to know when to stay in a bad work environment and when to run away from it as fast as you can. Nevertheless, everyone, even a bad boss, values the colleague they know will cover their back when the team comes under fire.

Your Character

With the three essential elements of character in mind—loyalty, transparency, and trustworthiness—ask yourself these six thought-provoking questions about your current working relationships. Your answers will help you develop an action plan for improving your skill at reputation management.

1. **If my name came up in a conversation among the leaders of my organization (or among my colleagues or clients), what would they say?** Will they mention your loyalty, transparency, and trustworthiness? Others will often comment on these overriding traits more than on your performance on a recent project.

2. **Can I list at least two occasions in the past few months where I displayed a high level of trustworthiness, honesty, and loyalty?** Do those traits generally guide your behavior, or do you struggle to make them a part of your daily character? Remember to keep the descriptors in your Blind Spot and your Facade panels in mind as you answer this question.

3. **Would people call me an optimist, a pessimist, or a mix of the two?** Do you consciously champion the work at hand, or is it hard work to maintain a positive attitude when the going gets tough? Anyone can whistle through a rose gar-

den. It takes more character to sing during a hard-fought battle.

4. **Do people approach me for advice and help?** Do they share both their triumphs and setbacks with you? In almost every group of human beings, one person serves as a Big Brother or Big Sister. People naturally gravitate toward the person they can trust as an honest and loyal confidant.

5. **Do I make my own voice heard?** It's important to be able to ask for advice and help, and equally important to share your accomplishments and failures. Others not only feel flattered when you share your innermost thoughts and feelings, they will do whatever they can to help and support you.

6. **If I could change one aspect of the way I relate to other people at work, what would it be?** Do you need to make a more conscious effort to become more trustworthy, transparent, and loyal? Everyone wants people with character on their team.

Regardless of how positively you answered these questions, you probably see some room for improvement.

Designing Your Character-Building Game Plan

To help clients consciously develop the sort of character they need to summon success in life and at work, my father, Organizational Management Consultant Patrick D. Curran, and I created a tool we call Your Power Bank© (see Figure 4–2).

No matter what you do for a living, and regardless of your

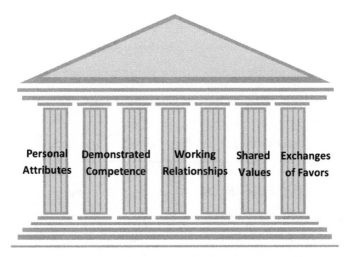

FIGURE 4-2 Your Power Bank

position in an organization, you can use this tool to enhance your position power. By "position power," I mean the power to influence others, whether you work for, with, or above them in your organization. The same applies to those you influence as a solo entrepreneur. It all starts with character.

Your Power Bank consists of five pillars that represent your history with your coworkers: your character, your competence, your relationships, your shared values, and the favors you have exchanged.

1. **Character**: These are your *personal attributes*. They include the way you present yourself, your drive, the credibility you have built with coworkers.
2. **Competence**: This refers to your *demonstrated competence*, your reputation as an expert in your field and your track record for getting things done.

3. **Relationships:** This refers to the quality of your *working relationships*. Strong workplace relationships are built by maintaining regular, open communication with one another and your ability to understand your coworkers' needs.

4. **Shared Values:** These are the values and norms you share with your coworkers both in the workplace and beyond.

5. **Exchanges of Favors:** Your ability, willingness, and track record for helping others typically determines whether others will help *you*.

Think of these pillars as safety deposit boxes where you add, store, and retrieve the currency you need to increase your influence. The more you invest, the more you withdraw. Like a savings account, the more regularly you make deposits, the more your account will grow.

TAKING STOCK

Identify three people with whom you need to develop excellent relationships in order to move forward in your career. For example, Matma selects her boss, Bob; the most senior member of her team, Cheri; and their Chief Technology Officer, Abdul.

Rate the five pillars of the Power Bank for each of these key relationships as High, Medium, or Low. *High* means that you are clear on the answers to this question and/or you are confident that this is an area of strength for the two of you. *Medium* means that you think that you do an okay job in this area with the other person or that you know a bit about them in regard to the topic. *Low* means that you are unclear about the answer to this area and/or you think this area is a weakness for the two of you.

After Matma takes some time to think deeply about her three key relationships, she comes up with the results below.

MATMA'S POWER BANK	THE THREE PEOPLE MOST CRITICAL TO YOUR CAREER EVOLUTION		
	Person #1 Bob	Person #2 Cheri	Person #3 Abdul
Personal Attributes	High	Low	Low
Demonstrated Competence	Medium	Low	Low
Working Relationship	High	Low	Low
Shared Norms/ Values	Medium	Low	High
Exchange of Favors	Low	Medium	Low

When you recreate the table and fill it out for yourself, the results will show you exactly where you need to invest more time and effort increasing your personal influence. You can then use this to develop your personal action plan.

Matma's action plan focuses on each area she has rated Low. With Bob, she looks for ways she can help him do his job better, and vice versa. For example, she asks if she can tutor a new member of the team, saving him time he can devote to more serious issues; in exchange, he invites her to accompany him to a training seminar on the Emotionally Intelligent Team. Cheri receives most of her attention, because Matma realizes how much she can benefit from Cheri's vast experience.

Spending more time with Cheri will enable Matma to demonstrate her trustworthiness and skill, thus opening the door for a more fruitful relationship based on their shared values. Abdul represents a different sort of challenge, because Matma does not interact with him every day. She must rely on Bob to convey her personal attributes and exceptional skills to his boss, but she can go directly to Abdul, offering to help make the case for increased funding for an important project, something she can do on her own time. Grateful for this offer, Abdul moves her up on his list of candidates for promotion.

I often coach clients on the use of the Power Bank. You can "hire" your own coach by asking your trusted confidant to help you maintain your objectivity and ensure that you do not get fooled by the traits that you identified earlier in the Facade and Blind Spot panels of the Johari Window.

Managing Your Power Bank's Deposits and Withdrawals

As you grow and manage your Power Bank, you want to make sure that you obey three basic rules of the game. You should always strive to:

1. **Become the "go-to" partner.** Be the magnet that draws people to your sphere of influence.
2. **Heed your organization's culture.** Respect the "way we do things around here."
3. **Maintain your integrity.** Remain true to your core values.

BECOME THE GO-TO PARTNER

Amazon exec Kelly Jo MacArthur relies on an interesting litmus test to tell her whether or not she is building the right kind of relationships within her organization. "I know I am leading well if people throughout our organization, not just on my team, come to me to problem-solve with complete trust that I will honor their beliefs and the organization's needs above my own." When people trust you to help them in strict confidence, without judging them harshly, they will beat an eager path to your door, not just with problems and questions about their work, but with their triumphs and successes. If you worry more about their careers than your own, they will return the favor tenfold.

This approach perfectly exemplifies one of the central tenets of good Power Bank management. Each person who comes into her sphere of influence makes a deposit. As the deposits accumulate (with interest), Kelly adds to her influence. By demonstrating her character, always linking who she is and what she does with the way she relates to people, she earns a reputation as a go-to partner. Whenever she needs to spend some of that currency when she herself needs help and support, people will quickly come to her aid.

Matma needs to work on this aspect of her character. If her boss and colleagues continue to see her as someone with unbridled ambition, who cares only about her own success, they will look elsewhere for help and support. Her sphere of influence will deflate to the point where people will actually take a little pleasure from her failures and setbacks. Opening up and sharing her vulnerabilities will attract people, not put them off. (This assumes, of course, that her organization's culture values this tenet. If yours doesn't, well, you might be in a toxic situation.)

HEED YOUR ORGANIZATION'S CULTURE

Sarah, a sales executive at a premier footwear and apparel company, disclosed to me how challenging she still finds it to voice her own diplomatic point of view, particularly in heated high-level meetings where she is often the only woman at the table. As we explored this career challenge, we saw that her upbringing contributed to her self-enforced silence when she disagreed with something someone had said in a meeting. As a child, her parents had insisted that she address all adults as Mr. and Mrs. and hold her tongue in their presence. "A good kid is seen, not heard." She even calls her in-laws Mr. and Mrs. Smith. Now that she finds herself thrust into a highly competitive and male-dominated work environment where the culture encourages people to speak their minds and engage in healthy conflict, she sits quietly as others energetically debate an issue, and when she does mumble a contribution, the man sitting next to her looks startled. "Did you say something, Sarah?"

I encouraged Sarah to deal with her reluctance to enter the fray during meetings by asking a man she trusted implicitly for his advice and support. It helped a lot. "A lesson I have learned from my male counterparts is that you have to make every statement with conviction and confidence, even if you are unsure, and then you must address the questions and encourage an open dialogue, never getting defensive." Her natural inclination, a basic component of her character, had schooled her to restrain herself in the presence of people she perceived as superiors. When she found herself working in a culture that dictated the opposite sort of behavior, she needed to heed the culture's values or deselect herself from the organization.

This issue can afflict men just as much as it does women. But women usually find it harder to fit into a culture that sometimes feels like a gladiator contest. A client in Dallas felt like the "odd man out" in what she called "testosterone-driven" planning meetings. I coached her to strengthen her Power Bank by talking frankly with the three men in her company who could do the most to forward her career. They loved it when she asked for their advice and promised to tone down the macho talk and do more to invite her opinions on important matters. The company's culture, it turned out, just needed a little tweaking.

Matma needs to step back and assess the values most prized by her organization's corporate culture. There, "the way we do things around here" includes a strong emphasis on emotionally intelligent teams, where people wear their hearts on their sleeves. Rather than playing the blame game when something goes wrong, people rally to devise innovative solutions. If Matma simply cannot learn to behave that way, she should consider moving to a company with a culture more aligned with her single-minded focus on personal success. However, a dog-eat-dog environment would probably not please her, either. I'd advise her to adapt her style or risk stalling her path to management.

Michael Morris, General Manager at Appirio, a global crowd-sourcing software-development community focused on the design, development, and data science that redefines business, sheds an additional insight into the relationship between an individual and their organization's management approach and culture: "If a candidate can't demonstrate some degree of clarity for the next five years of their career, it's a red flag. I am looking for potential hires to have a passion for what they are doing and where they are going. That passion has to align with the mission of our company, management, and culture." By the same token, you should assess a prospective employer's culture *before* you join the outfit. Will your passion and their mission make a good marriage?

MAINTAIN YOUR INTEGRITY

Regardless of the gap between your passion and your organization's mission, you must never, ever sacrifice your core values. Without a reputation for unflinching integrity, you cannot expect people to trust you completely. To put it another way, you must remain faithful to who you are as you do what you do to the very best of your ability. Otherwise, you can kiss your relationships goodbye. You can't feign a strong character. People will sense faked or superficial trust, honesty, and loyalty. I often tell clients that they should never forget the three most important aspects of relationship building: authenticity, authenticity, and authenticity.

Scott Fenton, Chief Information Officer and Vice President of River Wind Systems (An Intel Company), told me how early on in his career he resolved to present himself as C-suite material. Twenty-five years ago he was working at Tektronix, a company with a highly competitive culture. Although he saw himself as a future leader and concentrated on doing exceptional work, he found it difficult to form just the right relationships he needed to get ahead. He just couldn't find the voice he needed to express his "inner leader" to others. He described his early experiences with trying to speak up and speak out as "nerve wracking" because he felt so intimidated by his coworkers.

Over time, Scott managed to solve the problem through skillful networking and a growing sense of confidence in his own abilities. He found his voice by listening to his inner leader telling him to rely on who he was and what he did. Eventually, speaking in public did not make him so nervous. "If you are not feeling those pangs of growth, then you are probably not expanding yourself in the way that you need to if you see yourself eventually acquiring a senior-level position. If you want to get to the C-suite, it is mandatory that you gain tremendous confidence and extraordinary public speaking skills." Authenticity carried the day.

Matma need not cast off the traits that make her who she is and enable her to do what she does so well. Nevertheless, she should heed those "pangs of growth" and add relationship-enhancing traits to the ones that make her who she is: adding "reliable" and "supportive" to "self-sufficient, serious, reserved, calm, ambitious."

Wrapping Up

Each of us possesses our own unique character. A strong person needs certain qualities, such as trustworthiness, honesty, loyalty, integrity, empathy, and sensitivity to the needs of others. But we also develop our own special blend that makes us who we are, enables us to perform efficiently in our work, and allows us to build satisfying and productive relationships.

Select three people whose character you most admire and hire them to serve as "tellers" in your own Power Bank. You might pick a boss or mentor, a brother or sister, your mother or father, a world leader, or even a fictional hero or heroine. Then make a list of the four or five attributes they possess and you most admire. Do you own these traits? If so, to what extent do you display them on a daily basis? If not, what exactly can you do to acquire and sharpen them?

Here's an example from our friend Matma:

1. Character role model: Deepak Chopra.
2. Character traits I most admire: Knowledge, family loyalty, serenity, generosity of spirit, and willingness to share his knowledge with others.
3. Traits I share: Knowledge, family loyalty, and serenity. I should work on becoming more knowledgeable about group dynamics and find ways to extend more loyalty to my workmates.
4. Traits I need to develop: Generosity of spirit and a willingness to share my knowledge with others. Every morning on my way to work I will try to think of specific skills I can offer at least one person at work.

Imitation is not only the sincerest form of flattery, it is the surest way to acquire and to develop the character traits you need in order to achieve greater success in your life and career.

chapter five

Harmony: Orchestrating a Life While Pursuing Your Life's Work

Phillip has always taken care of the important people in his life. As the oldest of four brothers whose parents worked long hours in the family grocery business, he took on the role of cook, counselor, and surrogate parent for his three siblings. His experience as a one-man support group had helped fuel his success as a campaign manager for a host of high-profile New England politicians. Phillip's clients came to depend on him to run a well-oiled machine, something he seemed to do without ever getting flustered.

It came as a great surprise to clients, friends, and family when Phillip announced his decision to do something he had always considered much too selfish for someone who always put the welfare of others before his own well-being. He would, at long last, take a break from his secure career path and earn an MBA degree, a major step toward securing a university position teaching what he had learned on the campaign trail. Work and family obligations had always stifled this ambition, but somehow he had finally reached a point in his life where he vowed to set his professional life on a new track. He would limit his involvement in the campaign and go to graduate school at night. Still, the move gave him pause. Could someone who had always been there for everyone else finally be there for himself?

Many successful people question the meaning of their life at some point, often at many points, and find themselves wishing they had achieved more harmony between what they do for a living, what they do for their loved ones, and what they do for themselves. This can happen to anyone at any age. If it happens to *you*, what will you do? Will you seize this opportunity to take a hard look at your life and craft or blaze a different path that will help you feel more satisfied?

Composing Your Unique Harmony

You hear a lot about the work–life equation from career advisors, who suggest that life is a balancing act and advise that you need to place equal weight on both sides of the equation: a great career and a wonderful personal life. In my opinion, that way of thinking can lead to one of the most debilitating psychological problems of the modern era. It's what I call the "all doing, all being syndrome" (ADABS). The disease springs from the idea that you can have it all. But I'm sorry to report that no one, not even the bravest and smartest among us, can ever have it all, both a spectacular career and a perfect personal life all day, every day.

I prefer to think in terms of *harmony*. Jill may find harmony working sixty hours a week and spending weekends with her family. Jose may find it working thirty hours in his home office while being a stay-at-home dad. Each of us must follow our own drummer.

How about Phillip? For many years he found harmony serving others, but eventually the music stopped for him, forcing a long, hard look at his work–life balance. Selflessness, it turned out, had kept him from finding his own best self, and without his own deep personal fulfillment he could not keep on doing for others. An unhappy Phillip could not keep making everyone else happy. Seeking greater harmony was not a selfish act. Finding it would make him an even better caregiver and supporter.

But like so many of the success factors we have been discussing in this book, it's easier said than done. All the noise that attends our daily work and all the cacophony that erupts in our personal lives make it hard to hear our true calling. That's why it's so important to stop and listen for the music that beckons you forward.

Whenever I feel as if I'm pushing a boulder up a mountain and it's starting to fall back on me, I stop to listen for the music. The harder I work to keep my career moving upward, while putting even more effort into keeping my family safe and secure and happy, the more I feel the boulder pulling me downhill. When I do force myself to pause and take stock of the situation, I almost always find that I have come down with a case of ADABS. The best cure for that affliction? A large dose of harmony.

To find our special forms of harmony, Phillip and I must first recognize what ails us. The symptoms that indicate a need to change include trying to be all things to all people, acting on the unspoken belief that happiness can only come from doing what we always do, taking responsibility for everything that happens, and failing to seek the help of our teammates at work and at home. Let's take a look at what you need to do to be able to adopt a more harmonious mindset

Diagnosing ADABS

Over the years I have detected a common theme in the lives and careers of those I've coached. Now, these are intelligent, well-educated, and savvy professionals who possess a lot of life skills, but more often than not I found most of them in need of increasing their understanding of their own emotions. As we discussed in Chapter 4, Daniel Goleman explored the concept of Emotional Intelligence, a person's self-awareness with respect to human relationships and interactions. A deficit in this area often contributes to ADABS. Someone suffering from this syndrome thinks, "Since my success in the world depends on me and me alone, I must do everything myself." That sort of thinking may facilitate taking accountability for results in your life, but it can also turn you into an overcommitted, overworked, and very unhappy individual. Even the most talented one-person band can't keep playing all the instruments 24/7. Sooner or later, you wear yourself out while the success you so fervently desire slips further and further beyond the horizon. However, with a little more self-awareness and a higher level of Emotional Intelligence, you can treat, if not cure, the causes and symptoms of this career-stifling syndrome.

LISTEN TO WHAT YOUR ACTIONS SAY ABOUT YOU

In Chapter 1, leadership consultant Dr. Mary Ann O'Neil stressed the importance of matching our behavior to our values. In other words, when we do not know precisely where we stand on an issue, we should listen to what our behavior tells us. If Phillip feels unsure about his decision to move away from the political arena, he should look closely at how he feels and acts when he discusses an invitation to manage yet another election campaign. That queasiness in the pit of his stomach and his slumped shoulders are telling him he should think twice about accepting the job.

Enrica Carroll (remember her from Chapter 2?) shared with me a story about how she listened to what her actions were trying to tell her about her tendency to micromanage everything—and everyone—in her life. Looking closely at how micromanaging others did not reflect her belief in the importance of empowering those around her, she decided to make some important changes in the way she related to others: "Surrounding yourself with the right people is critical and enabling. But it also requires you to stop needing to do everything yourself, or insisting that it be done your way. It demands a leap of faith that others can do what you did and do it as well or better. Happily, I was finally able to take that leap."

The need to control everyone and everything in your world is a principal cause of ADABS. I have yet to meet a truly successful and happy control freak. Unmanageable people and unexpected events always get in their way.

LET GO OF YOUR DESIRE TO CONTROL EVERYTHING

Like the keys to success that we've looked at so far—motivation, confidence, risk-taking, and character—harmony is a state of mind. To build more of it into your life and work, you need to limit your desire to control everything that can affect your success. Paradoxically, you do need to exercise a certain amount of control, especially self-control, in order to gain success in anything. However, too much control can work against attaining your goal if it becomes a bad habit that makes people dread working with you. As with any bad habit, it can take a tremendous amount of time and willpower to get back on a healthier track. Just ask anyone who has ever tried to stop smoking or lose weight.

People like Enrica Carroll can often achieve an important self-realization by using a three-step process I often recommend to those suffering from the ill effects of ADABS:

> **Step One: Identify three instances in the recent past when you tried and failed to control an outcome.** Phillip listed three occasions during a recent campaign when he did work he should have delegated to a volunteer.
>
> **Step Two: Name the people in your sphere of influence who could have done a fine job doing what you tried to control.** Phillip admitted that he could easily have let the campaign's speechwriter, travel scheduler, and chauffer do the jobs he had hired them to do.

Step Three: Remind yourself that getting the right result matters more than the way you get it. Phillip would have written a different speech, booked Cleveland before Columbus, and driven on side streets rather than the freeway. So what?

Greater harmony comes almost naturally whenever you implement this three-step process. In Enrica's case, greater delegation made her and her teammates much happier on the job and a happier team. And Phillip found the campaign actually running more smoothly when he abandoned his need to keep his hands on every little detail. A terrific article in the *Harvard Business Review* sheds light on this topic. In "Management Time: Who's Got the Monkey?" authors William Oncken and Donald Wass discuss the old "command and control" era of management. This was when bosses kept their hands on all the controls and, as a result, ended up with every single problem on their own plates, or, as the authors put it, "with a huge gang of monkeys on their backs."[1] You can create a much happier and more productive workplace if you let people wrangle their own monkeys.

Team thinking can also provide a great antidote to an overriding need to control everything. I heard some good advice about this approach from Rahul Nawab, Founder of IQR Consulting in the Ahmedabad Area of India. He won "2014's Most Promising Entrepreneur in India," an honor bestowed by Asia Pacific Entrepreneurship Awards. In a far-ranging discussion about his success, Rahul offered me some good advice about letting go:

On the surface I wanted my team to have ownership on tasks, but I would quickly jump in and *fix* things. But later I realized that if I let go, it can actually be better than just jumping in to fix everything. The key here was a realization that my role is evolving and so will the team's role. As we are evolving, we need to ensure that there is a philosophy and a belief around the trust that ties us together.

You always find it much easier to surrender your need to control when you trust someone else on your team to do the job just as well as you would. And *team* isn't restricted to the workplace; your family is a team, and so is your circle of friends. Phillip should look at all the tasks he performs and ask himself two simple questions. "Who else could do this? Do I trust them to do it well? If so, let it go."

EVALUATE YOUR RELATIONSHIP BOUNDARIES

We all feel tugs on our time and attention from friends, family, colleagues, clients, and even perfect strangers. Finding harmony depends on drawing appropriate relationship boundaries that define "where I begin and you end." Boundaries separate acceptable and necessary demands from those that disrupt the harmony in our lives. Since Phillip had drawn almost no boundaries, he lost his "I" to all those people who expected him to do all and be all for them. When he started to set more self-fulfilling boundaries, he had to take specific relationships into account. For example, he decided he would drop anything he was doing to honor a request from his girlfriend but would not perform personal favors for any of his colleagues or clients. He also erected a fence around his personal life, taking less work home at nights and minimizing the occasions where he mixed business with pleasure.

Redrawing boundary lines can cause some initial problems, of course, as people who previously enjoyed total access to your time and attention now find their access restricted. In the early weeks of his boundary-setting campaign, the people in the campaign office expressed frustration when they had to do something the old Phillip would have done for them. But as time went by, they actually enjoyed and benefited from the opportunity to display their own talents and abilities. His girlfriend loved the new rules because Phillip has become much more available and attentive at home. You should spend time explaining your new boundaries in a positive way: "In order for us to accomplish our goals, I must set some new rules governing our interactions with each other." You can do everyone a big favor if you also help them create more effective relationship boundaries.

TAKING STOCK

In an effort to determine your susceptibility to ADABS, take a few minutes to answer the questions below and evaluate your relationship boundaries. You might discuss your evaluation with a few people in your sphere of influence, choosing those who will not feel offended if the discussion reveals a need to draw new boundaries with them. Rate your tendencies on a scale of 1 to 4 (1 = Never, 2 = Seldom, 3 = Often, 4 = Always).

- Do I frequently apologize for missing a deadline or failing to deliver on a promise?
- Do I feel powerful when other people rely on me more than they do on others who could provide the same support?

- Have I sacrificed my own needs in an effort to make other people happy?

Congratulations if you confidently said "Never" to all of these tendencies. Obviously, if you responded "Always" to any of them, you've got a serious case of ADABS and need to embark on a program to change your ways. If you rated any of them as "Often," you probably need to set some new boundaries. Even if you answered "Seldom," you may need to make some slight adjustments to a boundary. Keep in mind that you are seeking clues to the ways in which a lack of appropriate relationship boundaries have invited a certain amount of disharmony into your life.

A full-blown case of ADABS can severely impair your career. The harder you try to do it all and to be there for everyone all the time, the less you end up doing for anyone, especially yourself. You end up feeling exhausted, angry, and unhappy. Those around you feel short-changed and resentful. Before you begin treating a case of ADABS, you should ask yourself some penetrating questions about key issues that can contribute to a state of disharmony in your life.

ASKING THE TOUGH QUESTIONS ABOUT
Harmony

By now you know that I cannot silence the therapist in me, but even without my training in psychology I would strongly believe that our early experiences in life dramatically affect the way we think and behave as grown-ups. Our ideas of harmony and balance are also continually influenced by our mentors, heroes, and aspirational role models. These ten questions will transport you back to your formative years as well as your current role models for life inspiration and guidance.

1. **Did my parents or primary care providers maintain a degree of work–life harmony?** The models we encounter early in our lives greatly influence our behavior as adults. If we grew up in a chaotic household, we may recreate those same conditions when we strike out on our own. *And vice versa*.

2. **Did my parents amicably share household and family responsibilities or did one person go to work while the other stayed home?** The economic challenges that make it necessary for both partners in a relationship to work may require a major shift away from your experience with a stay-at-home Mom or Dad.

3. **Were my parents relatively calm and stress free, or did they often seem frenzied and stressed-out?** Financial and interpersonal problems can create an unsettling experience for a child, who, later in life, might accept, rather than try to solve, problems that cause disharmony.

4. **What values guided my family's approach to work and home life?** If parents stress their own careers over the welfare of their children, their children will often repeat that pattern in their own lives. Of course, the converse holds true as well.

5. **Who were my role models as I was growing up?** Sometimes a child finds someone outside the home to emulate, a friend's parent, a fictional character, or a teacher. The

more harmony a young person observes, the more likely he or she will strive for it later on.

6. **Do I find myself behaving like my mother, father, or other role models now that I'm an adult?** Look for both positive and negative behaviors you can't help repeating. Reflecting on the models you encountered earlier in your life and on the way you model behavior yourself can greatly reduce the likelihood that you will develop a bad case of ADABS.

7. **How has my upbringing influenced my definition of harmony?** Regardless of your earlier experiences, you can define harmony in your own terms and not just accept the models that affected you in the past.

8. **Do I continue to look for role models who might help me orchestrate greater harmony in my life?** It's never too late to study people who have found more fulfilling ways to live and work.

9. **Would the most important people in my life, both at work and at home, congratulate me on developing greater work–life harmony?** As always, feedback from people who care about you can help you see yourself more clearly.

10. **Do I make a conscientious effort to provide a good role model to others?** Taking accountability for the way you influence others seeking greater harmony can keep you focused on "walking the walk."

ACCEPT DIFFERENT WAYS TO PLAY THE TUNE

If you listen to a hundred performances of "The Star Spangled Banner," you will hear a hundred different ways to play or sing the national anthem, from Jose Feliciano's slow, heartfelt rendition sung at the 1968 World Series, to Jimmy Hendrix's wild electric guitar version played at Woodstock a year later. There's always more than one way to get a good result. Rahul Nawab explained how he takes advantage of diverse approaches when he assembles a team: "Organizing a team in such a way that everyone gets to work on interesting projects or pieces of projects is very important to keep a team motivated and for team members to reach beyond their potential. If the team can strike above their weight, we have a winning combination." In other words, he picks the instruments, lets his people learn to play them, and then sits back and enjoys an award-winning performance. He sets his mind on letting people achieve harmony without a conductor waving a baton on every note.

Have you ever thought or said, "It's my way or the highway?" Nothing disrupts harmony more than an overgrown human ego. You know the old saying, "There is no I in T-E-A-M." Vice President and Managing Director of Los Angeles–based R/GA Advertising Agency Josh Mandel disclosed his particular struggle in this regard: "I suffer from the desire to be all things to all people, mainly because of my self-perception, my desire to be seen as someone who is smart, capable, and multifaceted. That doesn't mean that I try to do everything myself. I understand that everyone has their 'genius zone' and that problems are solved by groups who all bring diverse talents and abilities to the table. But I sometimes get too far on an idea or project because of my self-belief, when bringing in help earlier was the right thing to do."

It takes more self-confidence to rely on the help of others than it does to try and do everything on your own.

ADOPT AN ATTITUDE OF OWNERSHIP

Rahul's approach illustrates the value of setting appropriate boundaries for yourself, and thereby demonstrating to others that they can do the same. If Phillip watches the candidate for state office set smart boundaries, he sees more clearly how he might do that himself. It all comes down to your ownership. If you own accountability for the result, you will make adjustments as to who will do what and by when to get that result. Everyone involved in getting the result will also own the result, and sharing the workload will make it happen. When Phillip tells his family about changing course and going after an MBA, he discusses ways in which he must alter his work and life to make it happen. Of course, they offer to share the burden as much as they can. By owning the result himself, he encourages those who care about him to share ownership of it. The same happens when he informs his team and the candidate about his plans. They agree to adjust their workloads in ways that will support his dream.

MAKE EVERY SECOND COUNT

British Columbia's Nick Kellet, Co-Founder at List.ly, a company that brings needed structure to social content by combining crowdsourcing and interactive social polling, shared his secret to finding harmony: "I believe we follow the 'one percent rule.' It explains how we split our time between creating and consuming. One percent of the time we create, 9 percent we contribute/comment/shape, and 90 percent of the time we consume. I think this holds true for our ability to absorb change. Ninety percent of the time we consume existing processes, 9 percent we tweak and refine them, and 1 percent we actively seek out change and innovation."

Nick goes on to suggest that to gain true harmony we must reduce the time we merely go through the motions of life (consume and refine) and increase the time we do something creative. Poor Phillip. He has gotten so good at managing political campaigns that he can do it in his sleep. And he does just that, sleepwalking through his days at work, dreaming of that coveted MBA. When he decides to wake up and go back to school, he can feel the creative juices flowing in his veins.

To move in that direction, he will need to make some other creative changes in his approach to work and life. "Who can help me change tracks? Which people at work can pick up the slack if I cut back my hours? Which of my family members can take responsibility for some of my commitments at home?" The answers to such questions will contribute to more harmony in his work–life balance.

TAKING STOCK

Once you feel comfortable with the idea of delegating and sharing responsibilities, you can turn your attention to creating a team that supports your quest for harmony. A team approach not only combats the harmful effects of ADABS, it frees you to concentrate on what really matters. To help you think more deeply about creating a strong team, I invite you to play a version of Fantasy Football. Even if you know nothing about football, you'll quickly get the hang of this exercise. Pick a major project you hope to tackle in the coming months, perhaps taking a class in financial planning, or looking for a new job, or adding a major service or product to your business. Now, make a list of skilled people you could recruit to help you complete the project. This is your dream team.

You can play the same game to think up ways to create more harmony at home. Which friends or family members could work with you to complete a major project, such as a room renovation or a three-week vacation trip? What outside help might you recruit, perhaps a contractor or travel agent? Can you think of service providers with whom you can barter for their time and expertise?

Knowing that I needed help getting my book published, I recruited a literary agent and writing collaborator to help me fulfill the dream. Eventually, a great publisher and editor joined the team. With my team in place, I could focus my time and energy on what I do best, creating content for the book. Yes, I could have done it alone and self-published my book. But I'm glad I decided to replace "I" with "we."

Assembling Team Trinity

It takes two to tango, but it takes three to create real harmony: you, your work, and your family (in the broadest sense of the word). Kerry McFeetors, a woman repeatedly voted one of the Fifty Most Influential Women in Radio, shared an experience that drove home a vital lesson about the need to get all three playing in concert. As Senior Vice President and General Sales Manager of Katz Radio Group, Kerry had learned early on that in order to succeed on a high level, she needed to master the art of delegation.

It took time for her to become a skilled delegator because she found it hard to relinquish what she called "the hero routine." She had become successful by performing heroic feats and she loved all the admiration and perks a hero enjoys. When she reached a senior level, however, she realized that no hero could do it all. For her, the solution involved delegating appropriate pieces of a project or major task but retaining "editorial rights." In other words, she learned to let go of the need to author all the work and got better results by editing the work of others. Not only does this approach add to her growth as a leader, it nurtures the growth of everyone on her team. Hello, harmony!

Ah, but this lesson seemed to fly out of her head the minute she crossed the threshold from work to home life. Despite the fact that she and her husband employed a full-time nanny to help care for three young children, Kerry continually failed to rely on her home team and developed a full-blown case of ABADS. It all came to a head during a hectic business trip when she received a phone call from her daughter's nursery school. "No one picked up your daughter today!" she was told. "You knew we were closing early."

Those words almost gave Kerry a heart attack. "In that moment, I felt like a complete failure. I failed my kid, embarrassed myself at the school, and looked very un-put-together to my business associates. In short, that made me cringe. Appearing stressed and not in control was in direct opposition to my usual style: highly effective, functioning on multiple levels at once, while making it all look doable."

After she got her heart rate back to normal, Kerry finally realized that she needed to apply to her home team the same art of delegation that worked so well at work. A good, strong dose of delegation almost instantly cured her case of ABADS. Now, her home team relies on a master family calendar that shows who does what and when. And here's the really cool bonus: smarter delegating afforded Kerry more time and energy to create quality time with her family.

Valerie Berset-Price, founder and Managing Director of Professional Passport, a consulting firm that specializes in international trouble-shooting and cross-cultural mediation for companies doing business on an international scale, described her particular approach to harmony:

> My husband is a stay-at-home father, and we share all tasks in a way that is non-gender specific. There is nothing he does I don't do, and *vice versa*. We trust each other fully and rely on each other entirely. My daughter is now at an age where she is also becoming my partner in crime, accompanying me to business meetings and handling some office chores for me. She knows that I need her to make it all happen and she finds pride in having a role to play in our success as a family and as entrepreneurs.

That family has written a beautiful piece of music. And each member knows the score and how to play the right instrument at the right time.

Wrapping Up

Fellow Portlandian Jackie Barretta published the wonderfully insightful book *Primal Teams*, which contains exercises for boosting team performance. Although she does not focus on harmony per se, she does emphasize the need to enhance what she calls "optimal emotions," the terrifically positive, "can do" feelings that inspire people to do their most creative and fulfilling work.

I want you to take an honest look at your emotions when you think about your team. Write down the names of the five to seven people who figure most prominently in your work and home life. You might include your boss, your most valued colleague at work, a key employee, a spouse or significant other, children, and a close personal friend.

For each member of your team, contemplate the specific ways in which that person contributes to (or detracts from) your sense of self-fulfillment, your success at work, and your happiness at home. How does that make you *feel*? I realize this might take you into some uncomfortable places if, say, your boss's behavior adversely affects your personal life or problems with your spouse make it hard for you to concentrate at work, but you will never find true harmony if you don't constantly evaluate the way your teammates add to or subtract from the music of your life.

Keep this list in a drawer and look at it every few months. Revise it, if necessary. Remember that harmony is not a single great performance; it's a constantly evolving work in progress.

chapter six

Vision: Connecting the Dots to Your Future

At the tender age of four, Carla could draw incredibly life-like pictures of animals, her favorite subjects. She entered her teens an accomplished painter. After a stint at the famed Royal Academy Art School, she left London for New York and settled into the artists' enclave in Brooklyn's Williamsburg neighborhood. Happy with her budding career, she spent her days working as a Metropolitan Museum of Art docent, her nights refining her talent with watercolors.

Then one night, while tidying up her little studio, she saw the blank walls and mismatched curtains that made her room look lifeless. An idea struck her. What if she wallpapered her room with her own watercolor prints and hung up curtains dyed to match the walls? That clever idea led eventually to envisioning a new career path. Her business offered fresh, eye-pleasing office and household wall and window coverings. Move over, Martha Stewart!

One step at a time, she fulfilled that vision and now runs her own business in Greenville, South Carolina, a major center for textile manufacturing. To connect the dots from idea to success, Carla tapped the business acumen of a former college roommate; borrowed some money from a local credit union; took her fair share of hard knocks, financially and psychologically; and tiptoed her way through all the usual business briars and brambles. This chapter shows you how someone like Carla, with a lot of talent in one area but little or no business background, can use strategic thinking to go from dreaming about a fulfilling life to actually leading it day by day.

Making the Case for Strategic Thinking

Strategic thinking paints a picture toward future success; tactical maneuvers get you there. It's all about connecting the dots between here and there. The late management consultant, writer, and educator Peter F. Drucker described strategic thinking as, ". . . the continuous process of making present entrepreneurial (risk-taking) decisions systematically and with the greatest knowledge of their futurity."[1] There's our old friend "risk" walking hand in hand with "future." They never follow a straight path because the dots can meander to the left and right. But they always move closer and closer to their destination. That's why they always invite their loyal companion "flexibility" to accompany them on their journey.

When I talk about vision, I always stress the fact that it does not mean that you lie awake at night dreaming about a better future, but that you draw a mental picture of a clear and achievable destination you can reach step by step (or dot by dot). That's strategic thinking. It's one of the most fundamental business challenges you'll ever face. Remember Matma, the aspiring manager we met in Chapter 4? She longed for everyone to see her as management material, but she did not see two major dots missing from that picture. The first dot was developing a more collaborative relationship with her coworkers. The second dot was progressing toward her desired promotion with much more patience. Once she started thinking more strategically and added those dots to her repertoire, she started moving toward that desired promotion.

Kea Meyers Duggan, Marketing and Volunteer Engagement Coordinator at Los Angeles Conservation Corps, highlights the need to think strategically in a world that can seem daunting and even hostile to someone in the early stages of a career, especially in a tough job market:

> How to act and be seen as strategic and visionary in my day-to-day work is an ongoing issue for me. Somehow, I end up in organizations that are very top-heavy. I am typically in a managerial or supervisory role, but I have no one to supervise. It's very difficult to learn and grow as a manager, become more strategic, and have a seat at the proverbial table when you are mired in the details of execution every single day. I jump at opportunities where I can offer strategic recommendations, but those opportunities are rare.

Whether you hope to climb the ladder at a Fortune 500 company or wish to grow a business of your own (or anything in between), you won't get far without some serious strategic thinking: "Where, exactly, do I want to be in five, ten, even fifteen years? What steps must I take to get there?" The rush of daily life and work can muddy the picture. Work, work, work, play, play, play, there's never enough time in the day to sit back and develop your vision of a more fulfilling future. That's why I advise clients to avoid what I call the "shiny-object syndrome," the tendency to get derailed from deliberately and steadily connecting the dots by all the interesting distractions that come our way. No matter how much fun they promise, they more often than not do not belong in the picture. That promotion that takes you away from what you really love to do? Forget about it. Or what about that fascinating new product that will take more time and money to develop than the business can afford? Strike it from your to-do list. Let your vision guide your daily decisions.

ASKING THE TOUGH QUESTIONS ABOUT
Your Future

As you sketch your vision on your drawing board, make sure you ask yourself these nine important questions that will help you convert a hazy idea of a rosy future into a colorful painting you can hang on your mental wall.

1. **Have I clarified my basic motivations?** You should have made some progress toward answering this question in Chapter 1. Now you should ask it with respect to your vision of the future.

2. **Does my vision reach far into the future?** A good vision does not encompass just one or three or five, or even ten years. Think thirty, forty, fifty!

3. **Who will I serve?** Obviously you will mention employers, colleagues, and customers, but think more expansively to include your community, your country, and perhaps even the world.

4. **Have I developed an effective communication plan?** People cannot join your team or hand you the right tools if you keep them in the dark about your needs and desires.

5. **Which tools will I need in order to fulfill my vision?** Some tools may lie within easy reach. Others may take time and effort and even a financial investment to acquire.

6. **Do I see all the dots I need to connect in order to get from where I am to where I want to go?** You should be able to pin down a dozen or so specific subgoals you need to reach before you arrive at your ultimate destination.

7. **Have I prepared contingency plans to address detours and setbacks along my path to the future?** You should always ask "What if?" from a negative perspective, thinking about what you will do if something does not turn out the way you imagined or wished it would.

8. **Do I define failure as a successful learning opportunity?** When you crash into a lemon tree, take time to gather up all the fallen fruit and figure out a way to make a great big pitcher of lemonade.

9. **Do I keep patience, perseverance, and professionalism by my side at all times?** You will never find more trustworthy companions on your road to success.

Business people ask these questions and others all the time, because every successful ongoing enterprise demands positive, resourceful answers to each and every one of them.

Going Back to the Drawing Board

Dreams are for sleepers. Visions are for the wide-eyed and alert. After Carla achieved her vision of running a thriving textile business, she found herself wondering about the next dots. "Where do I go now?" she asked herself. To answer that question, she needed to go back to the strategic drawing board, setting a new destination and imagining what steps she needed to take in order to get there. Anyone who sits down with a clean drawing board should keep four basic guidelines in mind: think long term, serve others, communicate your vision, and choose the right tools.

THINK LONG TERM

Once Carla envisioned an alluring future, she needed to consider all the dots she would need to connect to get from here to there. Doug Mendenhall, a real estate investor, shared with me his thoughts on Carla: "It is the label, 'She's so strategic,' that usually means she sees the bigger vision, the forest through the trees. So again, being 'strategic' in this sense is practicing being visionary." In other words, good strategic thinkers don't stroll through the woods looking at individual trees, they climb aboard a helicopter, from which vantage point they can see how all the individual trees form a forest. It takes time and effort to do that, not to mention a lot of mental toughness, patience, perseverance, occasional restraint and caution, and a willingness to sacrifice some short-term rewards (tapping one maple tree) in order to reap the long-term rewards of a bright future far down the road (a 50-acre maple-sugaring business). Oh, and throw in a lot of confidence, a high RQ, and all the other keys to success we are exploring in this book, especially flexibility, because the exact size and shape of the forest never turns out 100 percent the way you envisioned it.

As a first step toward a future where she would incorporate her own artwork into home and office décor, Carla drew up a one-year plan. For the next twelve months she would focus as much of her time and attention as possible on connecting the foundational set of dots. This included enrolling in a business-planning course at her local small business development center and beginning to trademark many of her favorite prints, as well as collecting cost estimates from textile manufacturers. It also involved joining entrepreneurial associations with members who started a product-based company. Also, she started doing market research, asking friends, family, and potential customers for advice about the products they would buy from her.

SERVE OTHERS

Visioning may strike you as a selfish act, but it's your future. Whether you offer tangible products, like Carla's line of wallpapers and curtains, or a service, like my training and coaching business, you must ultimately work for the satisfaction of colleagues and clients. If you don't serve others well, you'll see all your connected dots go up in smoke. Good news: When you make other people happy, you make yourself happy. As your grandmother may have told you, "What goes around comes around." That explains why Carla spent every waking minute trying to find out what people really needed, not just what she thought they needed. A strong dose of reality supplied by others can keep you from connecting dots that aren't really there. It helps you maintain a healthy perspective about your aspirations and makes it unlikely you will abandon your dream when you hit the inevitable bumps on the road to success.

Wind River Systems' Scott Fenton talked to me about applying the notion of service inside the walls of a corporation:

> If you are looking to become more strategic, focus on becoming a trusted advisor for your organization's leadership. Work to understand what is important to them, then help them problem-solve. And build those relationships over time. I worked to learn something about every department of the organizations I have been a part of so I would be sure to offer counsel that took into account each dimension of our business's total landscape.

Scott makes daily deposits in his Power Bank (see Chapter 4) in order to move further toward his vision of himself as a corporate leader. To him, leadership means serving others. You can only serve yourself by serving those you lead.

COMMUNICATE YOUR VISION

Do you openly share your vision with the important people in your life? It surprises me that so many people keep their dreams of a better future to themselves, as if talking about their innermost desires would make them seem foolish or starry-eyed. After all, when you share a treasured dream, you risk someone poking

fun at or even stomping on it. "You want to be the Chief Financial Officer at a Fortune 100 company? You've got to be kidding!"

And on the flip side, others of us worry that the failure to
connect our dots to the future could reflect a certain amount of
ineptness or strength—as if everyone else has somehow figured
out their big vision for themselves. Either way, you cannot let
such doubts and worries deter you from working toward com-
municating your vision to others. How else can they help you
make your vision a reality? I know from experience that letting
others know your dreams will earn you more respect and encouragement than you can realize. Suddenly, doors begin to open,
dots begin to connect, and the path to tomorrow grows a bit more
navigable every day.

In Carla's case, she talked a great deal about her idea and
asked a great many people what they thought of it. All that communication paid off; it helped her finalize her company's tagline,
"Whimsical Art for Windows and Walls," and its mission statement: "To create and sell soul-stirring window and wall art for
the home and office."

Now she could convey something more concrete to others.
Friends and family, mentors and peers, and prospective suppliers
and customers eagerly gave her their two-cents' worth of
advice—and a million dollars' worth of help. Dot connected to
dot, connected to dot, connected to dot, . . .

The same holds true in the corporate world. Appirio's Michael Morris told me how much he values strategic communication. "You have to have great communication skills to be a
successful strategist. You have to be able to understand what others are thinking and feeling." Michael's observation highlights
the fact that communication is a two-way street. You need to tell

others about your vision, but you also need to listen carefully to what they say about it. Hello, reality.

According to Kelly Douglas, CEO of Itzy Ritzy, a children's accessories company, strategic thinking and communication begin even before your vision starts to take shape. Everything you say and hear about your work can end up in your big box of dots. Kelly began her career as a consultant at the management consulting firm Accenture, where she "played the game," by giving her employer the impression that she would happily end her days in service of the corporation, even though she was already feeling that she might one day strike out on her own:

> This is not to be interpreted as deceit or deception; you have to be committed in terms of working harder and smarter than your counterparts, always taking on more challenges, keeping a positive attitude, seeking out professional growth, making your boss's job easier, and overdelivering every time. By working like this, people will see you as on the partner track, even if you decide not to go that route. At least you will have the option if your career goals or family plans change.

The relationships she formed and traits she exhibited in the corporate workplace became valuable dots down the line when she started her own company.

CHOOSE THE RIGHT TOOLS

As I have stressed so often in this book, one size does not fit all. The visioning tools that work for me might not work for you, and vice versa. However, as you practice the art of strategic thinking, you will learn how to select the right tools for the job. Every quest for a vision requires the proper equipment, as Lieutenant Colonel (Ret.) Pete Rooks, who heads up the Leadership Development Program at the University of Portland, explained when he introduced me to John Calvin Maxwell's Rule of 5. According to Maxwell, well-known leadership expert, author, and pastor: "Picture a tree in your backyard that needs to be cut down. If you grab an axe and take five good swings at the tree each day, eventually you will chop it down. It may take a month to fell a small tree, while a big tree may take years to topple. The size of the tree isn't the issue; the real question is whether or not you diligently take five swings at it every day."[2] Rooks elaborated on this: "If you can't afford the time and energy to do it with a small tool, consider switching to a more powerful one—a big axe or even a chain saw." The same applies to connecting the dots to accomplish your vision.

In the previous chapter, we explored the subjects of sharing, delegating, and team building. Those same tools apply to visioning. Carla already possessed some crucial tools, in particular her talent and passion for painting, so she needed to think hard about all the other tools she would need. In the end, she assembled a virtual team that included a professor who could teach her business planning, manufacturers who could give her information about the cost and availability of a wide range of materials, an intellectual property attorney who could help protect her trademark rights, as well as friends, family, and potential customers. She started with a little hatchet and ended up with a toolbox full of other powerful tools that helped her get to where she wanted to go as effectively and efficiently as possible. It didn't take her long to chop her big oak tree into a nice stack of firewood that could keep her warm for years and years to come.

TAKING STOCK

Imagine that you have been invited to prepare and deliver a speech describing your vision for your career a few years down the road. Don't worry, I'm not going to ask you to step up to the microphone and inspire a roomful of strangers with a stirring presentation, but I do want you to take a sheet of paper or open up a fresh Word document and outline a ten-minute talk about how you see yourself working and living five years from now. Use the four essential ingredients—think long term, serve others, communicate your vision, and choose the right tools—as the major heading in the outline of your speech.

Under each heading write at least three or four major points you would make as you present your speech. Under "Think Long Term," you should list four or five specific objectives you wish to accomplish for your work and life (Carla might begin with "A business of my own that enables me to make a comfortable living using my artistic talent"). Do the same for "Serve Others" (Carla might include " Making people happier by brightening their homes and offices"). Keep going with "Communicate Your Vision" (Carla never stopped talking about her vision with the people she invited onto her virtual team) and "Choose the Right Tools" (Carla stayed abreast of the latest trends for consumer product goods entrepreneurs).

Adapting to Surprises

Helmuth von Moltke, an eighteenth-century Prussian general who wrote extensively on the art of war, advanced the idea that no strategy survives the first encounter with the enemy. In other words, all your best-laid plans must adapt to the surprises that occur the instant you put your strategy into action. This does not render visioning useless, but it does make it absolutely necessary to develop contingency plans for the times when Murphy's Law comes into play: "If anything bad can happen, it will happen, and at the worst possible moment." In order to adapt to the many surprises as you connect your dots, you can follow a few proven rules for correcting your course.

QUESTION EVERYTHING

Carmen Voillequé, co-founder of Strategic Arts and Sciences, a firm that provides advanced strategic visioning, planning, and coaching for organizations and networks, has inspired me. Her book *Evolutionaries: Transformational Leadership: The Missing Link in Your Organizational Chart* has influenced my development as a leader. She advises me to never stop asking questions as I design and implement my career strategy. Questioning can help you move from one dot to another because it teases out the negative and unexpected consequences of your tactical moves. The insights you gain will help you correct your course. In an interview with her, Carmen gave an example:

> Whether you are a new employee at the bottom of the organizational chart or the CEO, I guarantee that you are not asking

enough questions. In fact, the higher we progress in our careers, the less we seem to ask. But asking questions is the number one way that you can obtain information, especially negative information. The better you are at encouraging negative information to flow upward, the better you will be at troubleshooting customer and employee problems, heading key complaints off at the pass, and preempting destructive conflict in your organization.

I agree with Carmen that a knack for questioning can prevent a lot of misery in all aspects of your life, both at work and at home, because it assists you in staying ahead of any surprises and allows you time to plan ahead for necessary adaptations in your strategic planning.

WELCOME LIFE'S LEMONS

Some surprises, such as an unexpected job offer or promotion, will delight you. Others, such as getting unexpectedly laid off from your job or the sudden defection of a key business partner, will knock you for a loop. If life hands you a tasty plum, thank your lucky stars. If it hands you a lemon, whip up a glass of lemonade. No matter how many questions you ask, you must keep connecting your dots, while being open to the answers you receive and integrating that new direction into your adapted future plans. Carmen pointed out that it all comes down to whether you let an unwelcome surprise render you powerless or you take charge of what happens next:

Whether you are a "glass half-empty" or a "glass half-full" kind of personality, the key to success is a belief in *agency*—in your power to change the future and your role in it. Whether an optimist or a pessimist, a Pollyanna or a realist, the most successful people in the world are those who operate under the assumption of "high agency." Agency produces desired results. We must believe in our ability to influence others, change our situation, and improve the future.

Doesn't this sound a lot like being accountable? No matter how many lemons life hands you, only you can decide what to do with them.

TAKING STOCK

You know the saying, "Every problem is an opportunity in disguise"? We pay a lot of lip service to that saying, but it's not so easy to put it into practice. This exercise should help you take a close look at a problem and convert it from an irrevocable setback to a springboard to success.

Choose three major problems you have encountered in the past, ones that really upset or even derailed you. Describe what happened next. Did they paralyze you with anguish, or did you take immediate steps to deal with them? How did you resolve the problems? Did they cause long-term damage to your career? If you could turn back the clock, would you have done anything differently in order to make the most of the bad situation?

Here's an example to stimulate your thinking. Carla had

been moving steadily toward fulfilling her dream of running an innovative wall and window covering company when the economy took a nosedive and many potential customers could no longer afford the luxury of redecorating with Carla's painting-inspired products. What questions should she have asked herself before the economic collapse that would have kept it from blindsiding her? What adaptations might she have made to deal with the possibility? Have you thought about calamities that might threaten your own strategy? Write down some possibilities before you read what Carla did.

Wait for it . . .

Carla took a job on the manufacturing floor at an outdoor sporting shoe company, where she spent a year and a half learning a lot about footwear design. When the company bought her idea to develop a line of canvas shoes with designs similar to the ones she had developed for her own company, she earned a big bonus, which she used to get her company up and running again.

As you set about connecting the dots to your future, the individual trees may change, but you should not let that distract you from seeing the forest. Strategic thinking can prevent surprises from paralyzing you and get you back on track.

REDUCE SURPRISES BY STUDYING THE COMPETITION

A good strategist avoids surprises by getting inside the head of the enemy. Leadership expert Pete Rooks taught me that the odds of success increase when we know our competitors as well as we know ourselves. He drew this insight from Sun Tzu's *The Art of War*: "It is said that if you know your enemies and know yourself, you will not be imperiled in a hundred battles; if you do not know your enemies but do know yourself, you will win one and lose one; if you do not know your enemies nor yourself, you will be imperiled in every single battle."[3]

In Carla's case, she spent time studying her competition in order to reduce any surprises when she finally brought her first product to market. She had dismissed conventional wallpapers and drapes as too bland and uninteresting, but some careful research convinced her that most of her potential customers lacked her penchant for flashy art. That led her to rethink her initial offering, replacing extremely bright abstract artwork with more serene watercolors.

TAKING STOCK

Over the years, I have delivered television segments and speeches, mostly on the subjects of success, leadership, and business. Interestingly, most questions I get from my audiences concern the setbacks people encounter along the path to success. They wonder how I coped with major setbacks and disappointments. How did I bounce back from a defeat?

Emotions play an important role in our ability to conquer setbacks. Think about three occasions when your strategy did not go as planned, when some unexpected event set you back and forced you to take an entirely different path. For each of these setbacks I want you to answer three questions.

1. How did it make me *feel*? Did I feel disappointed, angry, depressed, or vengeful? Or did I react with

more positive emotions and in a relatively calm manner?

2. Could I have made better decisions about going forward if I had replaced negative emotions with more
positive ones? Would laughing in the face of defeat
have served me better than breaking down in tears?

3. How do I feel about the setback now? Did I turn the
problem into an opportunity, or did I let it push me
onto a path I wish I had not taken?

Your answers will help you stress positive steps you can
take to overcome setbacks and surprises. We all tend to get
unhappy when something bad happens, but more self-awareness about our emotions can help us keep moving forward,
even if we need to modify our path—remember, flexibility is
your friend—and connect some dots we did not see.

MAINTAIN YOUR CORE VALUES

No matter how unexpected the surprises you meet along your
path to success, you can navigate through them if you regroup
around your core values. Those values not only provide a rock-
solid foundation for strategic thinking, they help you stay the
course when circumstances throw up roadblocks. Take a few
minutes to review the core values you determined back in Chapter 1.

ACME Business Consultant Sara Fritsch does just that. This
boutique consulting firm crafts personalized business solutions
for a wide range of industries. Every day Sara reminds herself of

a bedrock value that guides her workday: "Keep your eyes on the ball at work."

> I have a very full life outside of work along with a husband and two young children, which could easily create distraction from career progression and results. I am careful about what I commit to, but once I commit I do whatever it takes to get things done. In order for me to have earned control over my schedule that makes everything work for me throughout my life, I am very aware of being 100 percent focused on the task at hand, and on the importance of delivering excellence every time.

Her focus not only allows her to tackle surprises when they occur, it prevents a lot of derailments because Sara is so focused on continually connecting the dots to her future goals each and every day.

Wrapping Up

Think of your current career strategy in terms of a business plan. A good business plan includes answers to Sinek's Golden Circle questions of *Why, How,* and *What*; it also includes *When.* Ask yourself: *Why* have I chosen this career? *How* am I delivering on my Why? *What* precisely do I do on the job? *When* will I have achieved my first major strategic goal?

Below you can answer each of those questions in a sentence or two. By way of example, consider Carla's responses:

Why? "I study and practice art to uncover unseen beauty

in our natural world. I have spent my life studying and practicing art and can imagine no other activity."

How? "I do this by observing nature and translating it onto various artistic mediums such as oil paint and watercolor prints."

What? "I have been painting for my own satisfaction but would like to devote more time to tailoring my art to the needs of other people. A wall and window covering business would allow me to do that."

When? "I will have reached my first major goal when my business employs at least five other people and is netting $300,000 in sales."

Of course, as you keep connecting the dots to your future you will encounter many surprises along the road. You will find it easier to deal with them if you maintain a sense of control over your own fate, take full accountability for your future, and remain optimistic, flexible, and patient every step of the way.

chapter seven

Community: Designing Your Powerful Network

Immediately following graduation from college, Stephen inherited his family's Minneapolis-based insurance business. Over the next five years, he successfully grew the business from a one-policy life insurance company to a diversified firm offering a full stable of financial planning services. Independent and determined to remain continuously in the top 10 percent of every category in his customer satisfaction survey, Stephen prided himself on hiring only the best and brightest for his firm's staff of ten. Why, then, did his company suffer an alarming rate of turnover?

Ironically, Stephen's fierce independence, one of his strengths, had become a weakness. When he decided to hire someone, he relied solely on his gut instinct and never bothered to seek the opinion of a peer or mentor. For whatever psychological reasons, Stephen built walls instead of bridges. When he made a poor hiring decision, he could only blame himself. If he had discussed the matter with a confidante, he or she might have pointed out the flaws in the candidate. A second opinion might have convinced him not to hire the person in the first place.

Stephen had never considered building a network of people whose advice and opinions would help him make better business decisions. He had never joined any local professional associations and knew few other businesspeople in town. Stephen may have won his independence, but he had lost the benefits of belonging to a community of peers, mentors, and advisors who could provide much-needed referrals, reality checks, and tips for improving profitability and growing a business, not to mention giving him a sense of belonging to something bigger than his own little corner of the world.

If it takes a village to raise a child, it takes a network to make a career click. Some of us, like Stephen, worry that seeking help and support signals weakness and exposes our vulnerabilities in a way that makes us seem less competent. Nothing could be further from the truth. People love to help others succeed. When someone does you a favor, and you do them a favor in return, you both come out ahead. A win–win!

In this chapter we will equate designing a network with joining and expanding the "community" in which we live our lives and pursue our careers. This community may include business colleagues and competitors (yes, competitors), as well as mentors, teachers, advisors, and immediate and extended family members. This broad concept of networking can even include the city or town in which we live, our country, and the world at large. When we build strong bonds with our community, we create a safe haven for the sharing of ideas, concerns, and talents.

Facebook and Twitter and LinkedIn have made it possible to build far-flung communities by enabling us to connect continuously with people, both personally and professionally, but no gadget or website will ever replace the human need to build and cultivate mutually beneficial relationships face to face. When we do that, we assemble an army of comrades in arms who will do whatever they can to ensure our success, and vice versa. The Golden Rule applies. If we "do unto others" with our help and support, they will do likewise in our hour of need.

When we ignore the need for a larger community on which we can rely when we need something that will promote our professional and personal success, we court failure in both arenas. Stephen may start out like gangbusters, growing his business and making a lot of money, but sooner or later he will encounter a business problem or opportunity where someone from his network could have saved him a lot of time, money, and anguish.

A powerful network involves more than people helping people. It provides security, safety, and a keen sense of belonging that mean every bit as much as a big paycheck. Most of my clients, especially younger workers, tell me they want more meaning in their lives. Nothing can better satisfy that yearning than designing a powerful network, making friends wherever you go, joining clubs and professional associations, volunteering for charitable work, or actively participating in a spiritual or religious organization.

All of the successful people I know value their networks highly. Some cast their nets far and wide, while others develop smaller, more focused communities. For me, community means not just my family, friends, and professional business connections, but also my pro bono training clients, which include such nonprofit groups as Girls Who Code, Girls Inc., and the Junior League. These experiences have helped me satisfy my desire to serve emerging female leaders and they have afforded me friendships from which I will enjoy the rest of my life.

Networking Your Own Special Way

Like all good things in life, networking comes in many shapes and sizes. My brother Kevin, a genetics professor in the morning and a sailor in the afternoon, has a powerful network that consists of his science peers and his sailing buddies. Internationally connected customer service guru John Goodman's network spans continents. For some, their network is at the scale of a large organization, while for others it involves a handful of clients and suppliers associated with a small business. And, while corporations provide a built-in community, entrepreneurs must forge one on their own.

A network is a must, and it's up to you to populate your own. Who will you choose? When training and coaching, I like to keep it simple by urging my clients to understand what they do for others, and what others do for them. The answer to that question will tell you a lot about the size and shape of the ideal network for you.

While "Do unto others as you would have them do unto you" is a universal principle, it plays out differently in each of our lives. The way you practice that principle and use it to strengthen your network depends on the core values you clarified in Chapter 1's

Vital Dreams Detector and your Career Clarity Circle. It derives from your unique nature, background, education, talent, and experience. Nevertheless, the way you shape and participate in your network should always follow three basic rules: invest in the welfare of others, consider your own need for support, and tailor your network to your special talent.

INVEST IN THE WELFARE OF OTHERS

Of all the traits you need to succeed in life, powerful motivation ranks near the top of the list. Serving the needs of others rewards the self much more than selfishness ever will. That principle influences their interactions with other people. Intel exec Doug Fisher, whom we first met in Chapter 2, recently remarked to me, "It takes time to mentor, influence, and change lives. Being a leader is about people, and for me this means creating an environment where I have genuine interactions with employees at all levels in the organization. This means being truly interested in others, listening and believing you can learn from them as much as they can learn from you." Doug practices what he believes, refusing to seal himself off in an executive suite and preferring, instead, to work with people in open spaces where he can easily connect with them, and vice versa. The more he serves his people, the more they serve his needs and the company's interests.

CONSIDER YOUR OWN NEED FOR SUPPORT

Think of your network as two sides of a valuable coin. On one side you give; on the other you receive. Too often, we do not fully appreciate the side that needs support. Philadelphia's Tyrrell Schmidt, former Global Head of Segment Strategy and Marketing in the healthcare industry, didn't fully grasp the true value of her community until her employer moved her and her family to the other side of the globe. "For me, moving abroad raised the bar and meant settling kids into a totally different environment while settling myself into a new job in a new country. Finding a support network is important in navigating those challenges." This experience reminded Tyrrell that a strong community could help her and her family negotiate a major transition.

Growing up, we take communities for granted. We receive affection and friendship, schooling and mentoring, and food and shelter without giving much thought to how others fulfill our needs. As adults, however, we must make a conscious effort to join the communities that will provide the personal and professional sustenance we need. Doing that involves more than saying hello to people as you commute from home to office. This limited view of community cannot provide the support you need.

It's not easy to know when you need to seek support for yourself. Amazon's Kelly Jo MacArthur, introduced in Chapter 4, shared this observation: "I have built a personal board of advisors made up of men and women, older and younger. Whenever I am going through a big career decision, I will talk to most of them for feedback. Sometimes I may seek advice, but often I find they just reflect you back upon yourself so you can see yourself more clearly." Colleagues, mentors and experts give you support and constructive criticism; these individuals give you a clearer view of yourself. Stephen plays eighteen holes of golf with clients and fellow financial advisors once a week. He so enjoys the camaraderie of fellow members at the Fairview Golf Club that he volunteers on the club's social committee, where he has met several local business men and women who have become sounding boards whenever he needs professional advice.

TAILOR YOUR NETWORK TO YOUR SPECIAL TALENT

We serve effectively in areas where we can apply our special talent. If you like to play music and strum a mean guitar, you might offer to teach classes at the local library. Or, you might use your accounting skills to prepare tax returns for senior citizens. The mother of a teenager in your guitar class may end up connecting you to her best friend, a marketing consultant who can help you with a new ad campaign in exchange for teaching her son some advanced guitar techniques. Or a tax preparation client who once ran the human resources department at the local community college may become a terrific evaluator of prospective hires. If Stephen had consulted with her, the turnover at his firm would have been much lower. My colleague, *Inc.*, *Forbes*, *Fast Company*, and *Success* magazine contributor Laura Garnett, calls it tapping into our Zone of Genius™. For Stephen, his genius for financial analysis and retirement planning transferred beautifully to a one-night-per-week gig providing pro bono services to local fire and police departments. There he met young men and women who mentioned his service to their parents, many of whom eventually became paying clients.

TAKING STOCK

Welcome to our Talent Show. No matter what you do for a living, no matter your level of education or your experience in life, you possess a special talent. Pick one, whether it's as high-flying as a knack for rocket science or as down-to-earth as vegetable gardening. Then answer these questions on a separate sheet of paper:

- What community do I wish to join?
- In what three ways can I contribute to the community?
- What three benefits might I gain from the community?

Remember to think of the community as your powerful network. Start close to home, selecting a local community, such as other rocket scientists in local colleges and universities or gardeners in your neck of the woods. Then, think about moving outward, like the ripples in a pond, expanding your network to the state, national, even global level. Starting locally takes little time and energy, and the simple act of joining or creating a community at the local level can eventually lead to involvement at the national level. Just remember, baby steps are the key.

Think the same way when you imagine the benefits you hope to derive from participating in a community. Start with a modest and easily accomplished goal, such as making several new friends, then add a somewhat more ambitious goal, such as bartering your talent for much-needed financial advice, and finally set your sights on a supersized one, such as a partnership or merger with another person or company.

Communities function like living, breathing organisms. They come to life, they thrive, they age well or badly, and sometimes die. Make sure you do everything you can to keep yours healthy by investing not just your time but also your heart in their continued growth and well-being. You can grow so comfortably in a community that you start taking it for granted, but, as with all relationships, it takes some thoughtful effort to keep it vibrant and alive.

ASKING THE TOUGH QUESTIONS ABOUT
Networking

Whether your current community consists of you and a few racquetball partners, the local Chamber of Commerce, or the United States House of Representatives, you should continually assess your current and long-term professional needs and areas of desired service. These seven questions will help you evaluate your current approach to designing a powerful network:

1. **Do I broadly define what I mean by community?** For example, in any business your competitors are part of your extended professional community. You can teach and learn a lot from a professional or trade association.
2. **Whom do I serve?** Ask yourself if you have been attracting, building, and participating in communities at a level that satisfies the needs of others.
3. **Who serves me?** Explore the ways in which you benefit from each of your community engagements.
4. **Can I serve my community better if I engage more fully?** You may think you cannot afford the time to get more involved, when, in fact, you lose a lot of opportunities because you fail to engage sufficiently with your community.

5. **Can my community better serve me if I engage more fully?** Full engagement affords you opportunities to get what you need from your community.

6. **What can I do to serve others more fully?** Assume more of a leadership role in your community, serving on its Board or on an important committee.

7. **Should I look for or start a new community?** If you and a given community do not make a good match, look for a new one.

Evolving Your Network

Whether you think of your network as a river you ride with other people toward a sea of success or as a pond into which you drop a pebble whose ripples expand ever outward, your involvement with your community should constantly evolve. As your abilities deepen and your needs evolve, so must your network.

IDENTIFY THE RIPPLES

Stephen dropped his pebble into the pond when he joined the Fairview Golf Club. There he met a retired executive who suggested that Stephen donate some time helping first responders (police officers and firefighters) with financial and tax planning. That new ripple carried him to the local Senior Center, where a pro bono client urged him to join the National Association of Insurance and Financial Advisors (NAIFA). Involvement with NAIFA at the local level carried him to the national convention, where he conducted a workshop on community volunteerism. He made friends and picked up clients and professional contacts as his engagement with NAIFA deepened. This happened because he delivers exceptional service to others.

Think about ways you can create a similar ripple effect in your life and work, looking for opportunities to expand your sense of community beyond your own small corner. When you reach the edge of your own small pond, look for bigger bodies of water further from home.

You will discover that you can receive as well as give exceptional service. Stephen's workshop at the national NAIFA convention resulted in an invitation to write articles for the organization's newsletter. Readers liked his ideas so much that he won fans. One of those fans, Jill, owned a financial planning company in Iowa, and became Stephen's partner in a chain of financial planning offices. The Stephen-and-Jill Show has taken it on the road in six Midwestern states—and Stephen has created a panel of advisors (including staff members) to help interview new hires. Harder for the prospective employee (three separate interviews), for sure, but much better for the organization!

CONNECT NEEDS WITH SKILLS

We tend to gravitate toward people with similar backgrounds and interests. At first, we may interact with them purely as business associates, but over time they may become true friends. Janet Salazar, CEO and founder of IMPACT Leadership 21, a platform committed to transforming women's global leadership at the highest level of influence, told me how her mentor, Judy Lerner, who received mentoring support from Gloria Steinem, taught her to seek out people with whom she could develop authentic friendships. Genuine friendship makes it easier to get the help and support a good mentor can provide, and it allows you to offer help and support in turn to others.

A community may consist of only two people, you and a mentor or you and a protégé. In either case, it's a two-way street involving an exchange of skills and needs. Ghost CEO's Christopher Flett put it bluntly: "The first thing you should ask someone whom you have met and believe to have great value to you is, 'How can I help you?' If they do not respond with the same question to you within the next ten minutes or so, drop them. They will merely serve as what I call 'boat anchors' to you. They simply don't have it 'going on'." In other words, you should seek out people to collaborate with who understand the give-and-take of relationships.

It's easy to see what a community offers you, but not so easy for the community to understand what you need from it. Most communities, especially larger ones, such NAIFA, make it easy for people to join them. Newcomers often remain anonymous, sitting in the back row and keeping a low profile, at least in the beginning. Stephen knew what he wanted from NAIFA (professional contacts, continuing education, and a chance to sharpen his social skills), but no one in the community will know that unless he conveys his intentions. In most cases, the larger community will consist of many smaller communities dedicated to specific issues. When you join one of those subcommunities, you automatically tell people what you want to gain from the association. Find your niche.

Your needs must draw upon their skills; your skills must serve their needs. You can solve this equation in a smaller group, where people will invite you to share your needs during the very first encounter. When Stephen volunteers to serve on a subcommittee researching online continuing education, his commitment communicates both his desires and needs. Now he has positioned himself to serve the greater good while simultaneously serving his own self-interest.

By the same token, you need to make the community aware of the skills you bring to the relationship. Your new associates cannot read your mind. Whatever your particular talent, such as public speaking, teaching, writing, finance, or public relations, tell your community about it. Otherwise, no one will benefit from what you can bring to the party.

KEEP YOUR NETWORK OPEN FOR SURPRISES

Sometimes you get the most from people who do not share your particular background and perspective. Henry Ahn, Executive Vice-President, Content Distribution and Marketing at Scripps Network Interactive, told me how he often benefits from a community in ways he never anticipated. "I have been fortunate to work for people who kept giving me responsibility and expanding my comfort zone to take greater risks. I used to be very much numbers focused, but now I look at business from more of a broad perspective, especially how to develop and maintain good relationships." He did not go looking for sharper social skills; they came looking for him as he took on challenging new responsibilities. Open yourself to the possibility that you can learn from people who may not at first seem to offer what you need. Opposites attract. And opposites can make great partners.

An article in *Forbes* cited research in the field of network science that indicates the power of an open, versus a closed, network:

Most people spend their careers in closed networks—networks of people who already know each other. People often stay in the same industry, the same religion, and the same political party. In a closed network, it's easier to get things done because you've built up trust, and you know all the shorthand terms and unspoken rules. It's comfortable because the group converges on the same ways of seeing the world that confirm your own."[1]

The article goes on to point out that, in contrast, open networks invite people with different backgrounds and interests and skills and need to benefit from each other. Open networks:

- Help form a more accurate view of the world (an isolated group makes more errors than a diverse group that receives a wider range of input).
- Facilitate the timing of information sharing (specialized subgroups convey new information more quickly to the entire community).
- Enhance the role of translator/connector between groups (an intermediary introduces an individual or subgroups to people who might otherwise never meet them).
- Generate more breakthrough ideas (a collection of people with different backgrounds and perspectives come up with more creative solutions than a team that consists only of people who share the same perspective).

The article concludes with the words of Apple founder, Steve Jobs, "You can't connect the dots looking forward; you can only connect them looking backwards. So you have to trust that the dots will somehow connect in your future." There you go. It's all about connecting the dots. The more diverse the dots, the merrier.

Peter Wilson, President of the Australian Human Resources Institute, told me a wonderful story that illustrates the power of getting help from someone who did not seem to make an ideal mentor. While serving as a senior executive at ANZ, one of the world's top 100 banks, Peter joined the Board of the Melbourne Tigers Basketball Club, a team that played in the National Basketball League in Australia. There he met Lindsay Gaze, the Tigers' head coach at the time. Famous throughout Australia, Gaze had coached or played in eight Olympics. One day, Peter casually mentioned to the famous coach that losing a high-paying position usually devastated older executives. Coach Gaze pointed out that even Michael Jordan, considered one of the greatest basketball players of all time, had been cut from his high school team. That fact stuck in Peter's mind and helped him cope with setbacks he later experienced in life.

Peter's unlikely mentor gave him another insight that has served him well in business over the years. During a particularly competitive game, Peter was sitting beside Coach Gaze on the bench. The Tigers had finally taken a seven-point lead. When the coach talked to his players during a time-out near the end of the game, Peter assumed he was congratulating them on their performance. When the coach returned from the huddle, he looked at Peter and exclaimed, "We can be very inventive at finding ways to lose from positions like this!" Sure enough, the Tigers ended up almost losing that game. Only a buzzer-beating basket won the day. Peter took a great business lesson home that day: Always keep your head in the game.

TAKING STOCK

Back in Chapter 6 we played Connect-the-Dots. Do you know about "six degrees of separation," the idea that only six dots separate you from any person you want or need to meet? Believe it or not, I could use that networking approach to meet the President of the United States. My friend Valerie referred me to my literary agent, Michael Snell, who introduced me to John Bernard, CEO of the Portland-based consulting company Mass Ingenuity. Through John, I could meet Michigan Governor Rick Snyder, who wrote the foreword for John's book, *Government that Works*, and through Governor Snyder I could connect with the President's Chief of Staff and, finally, to the President himself.

How could you use this networking technique to meet someone who could give a big boost to your career? Think in terms of the community ripple effect, moving from one friend to someone at the local then regional level, and then move into the statewide, national, or global arena. Pick your target, and then connect the dots. Start with the target in mind.

- **Contact #1:** A friend or close associate
- **Contact #2:** A friend of that friend (local)
- **Contact #3:** A friend of that friend's friend (regional)
- **Contact #4:** That new friend's friend (statewide)
- **Contact #5:** A friend of that friend (national)
- **Contact #6:** The target (global)

> You may not need to meet a global powerhouse to move your career along, but this is how you would if you wanted to.

Sustaining the Flow

Remember what Laura Garnett said earlier about getting into our Zone of Genius? Well, you've got to stay in the flow, continually enriching your relationships within the community. In the early stages of the relationship you and members of the community spend time getting to know each another. It's a lot like dating. You meet. You talk. You share. You grow comfortable with each other. Maybe you even fall in love. Everything goes swimmingly during the honeymoon phase of the relationship. Then you get a little bored. You gradually disengage. Eventually you divorce. But divorce is uncomfortable, sometimes downright ugly. How can you keep your marriage alive?

Keep active in the community. Refresh the relationship by joining different subgroups. Run for office. Serve as a one-person welcome wagon for new members. However, you may need to move to a new community. Stephen made the most of his NAIFA membership, giving a lot of himself and getting a lot back in return, but after he and his new partner set up their six-state mini-empire, he decided to devote more and more time to local and regional communities, such as the Chambers of Commerce in the towns where their new branches were located. His partner Jill now represents the company at national NAIFA conventions.

Figuring Out What It All Means

No man or woman is an island. Communities lend meaning to our lives, and we pump life and meaning into our communities. It's the old two-way street again. When I think about the ripple effect in terms of meaning, asking myself what I most value from a relationship with one of my communities (my close friends, my neighbors, my business associates and peers, Portland, Oregon, the good old U.S. of A., and the world at large), I get a little mushy because I cannot talk about any of them without expressing feelings with the words "love" and "happiness."

Even if you have never seen the Bill Murray film *Groundhog Day,* you can appreciate the moral of the story. Like Scrooge in Charles Dickens's famous novel, the main character, Phil, reaches an epiphany that changes him from a miserable, self-centered, and arrogant fool to a humble man capable of truly loving his fellow men and women. Forced to live the same day over and over and over in Punxsutawney, Pennsylvania, Phil gradually realizes that the more he serves the well-being of others, the happier he becomes. Finally, he gets the girl of his dreams by thinking more about what *she* wants and needs than about his own selfish desires. Life in the community changes him; and by changing himself, he becomes a more valuable member of the community. Love and happiness matter more than all the money and promotions in the world.

Wrapping Up

I want to shake up your definition of community by inviting you to design an imaginary open network that includes four unconventional members. Write down a name, explain why you have picked that person, and then think about how you might use the "six degrees of separation" technique to meet him or her (if only in your imagination). My selections might give you some ideas about folks you might want to put on your own list:

MY OPEN NETWORK

1. Malala Yousafzai, a Pakistani activist for female education and the youngest-ever Nobel laureate. I'd like to learn how she derives her strength and vision in the face of so much oppression and suffering.

2. Sheryl Sandberg, COO of Facebook, activist, and author of *Lean In*. I admire her dedication to leveling the playing field for women and men both professionally and domestically and would love to hear about her particular motivations and perspectives.

3. Katie Couric, who currently serves as Yahoo Global News Anchor, and a former television host on all Big Three television networks in the United States. I would love to know how she has navigated the cultures and politics of the largest media networks in our country and what keeps her on top of her game year in and year out.

4. Oprah Winfrey, American media proprietor, talk show host, actress, producer, and philanthropist. I would ask how she has remained grounded while working in the public limelight all these years, particularly during major disappointments and setbacks.

Your list should offer some clues about what you need from a community. After thinking through the exercise, come back to the real world and look for people and organizations that can fulfill those needs.

Influence: Mastering the Key to Effective Leadership

Everyone who came into contact with geneticist Jessica could see that she understood her lab's clinical trial program better than anyone else on her multidisciplinary team there. She put in fourteen-hour days, six days a week, not just in the lab, but traveling to speaking engagements around the world. Personally, her teammates and boss found her aloof and unengaged.

She knew her colleagues felt that way about her, but she couldn't help the fact that she felt far more comfortable peering into a microscope or presenting her latest findings to a large group of fellow scientists than socializing with her lab mates. When her team went out for pizza and beer and the conversation turned to personal matters, Jessica drew deeper into her shell. She never shared her feelings. Nor did she try to understand what made her colleagues tick. When Walter, a less-accomplished colleague, received a new research grant, she couldn't believe it. "He's just better at influencing the boss," she thought. "There's no room in science for trying to change the way people think."

Think again, Jessica. Influencing plays a role in *everything*, from who gets the bigger slice of the corporate budget to who drives the kids to soccer practice. Learn to expand your influencing repertoire or get used to taking a backseat to those who do it well.

Walking in Their Shoes

Do you want to win an election? Do you want to influence people to vote for you? Do you want to gain funding for a project? Then, influence your lab mates and your boss so they see you as the best possible candidate. In order to convince voters to cast their ballot for you, you must first and foremost try to see the situation from their point of view. That takes empathy, the humble act of walking in another person's shoes in order to see the world from their perspective. And true empathy involves a careful eye and a patient ear, watching and listening for the clues that reveal the other person's hopes and fears. If Jessica got to know her colleagues over a pint of lager and a pizza, sympathizing with their dreams and complaints while confessing her passion for a new line of research, she would greatly increase the odds that when it came time for her boss to allocate funding, her name would be on everyone's mind.

When you expand your understanding of what motivates other people (and vice versa), you position yourself as a person of influence. You "get" them; they "get" you. That mutual under-standing forms a bond of trust and respect that will help you help one another. It takes more than just slipping into their shoes. You must look into their hearts and (here's the hard part for people like Jessica) let them look into yours. Jessica worries, "If I let down my guard, people will see that I'm not nearly as confident and knowledgeable as I want them to think." Little does she know that her boss has been worrying that she acts more like a robot than a normal human being. If only she could let the people at the table in on her little secret. Her rival colleague might laugh and heave a sigh of relief. "I feel *exactly* the same way, Jess! This work is *so* complicated." Jessica's admission would make her seem humble and worthy of a chance to pursue her new line of inquiry. What she fears as a roadblock to her advancement would actually influence others to help her move forward. With a little empathy, she would turn an imagined roadblock into a bridge.

Observing Effective Influencers

Who has won your admiration for their ability to influence the people around them, including yourself? I would pick my friends Kerry, Bruce, and Steve, who bring tremendous wisdom, cha-risma, and good humor to even the most difficult situations. They can always spare time for a friend in need. When I talk with them, I receive their full attention. They ask astute questions that help me focus and express my thoughts. They "get" me. As a re-sult, I listen carefully to their observations and advice. They in-fluence the way I act. When it comes to the gentle art of influence, they do it with style.

IDENTIFY THEIR SIGNATURE STYLE

What exactly does an artful influencer do? As with so many aspects of life, each brings a unique mix of talent and behavior to the party. Our friend from Chapter 4, Scott Fenton, shared his experience with a gifted persuader:

> A pivotal person in my career was CEO Matt Chapman at Concentrex/Harland Financial Solutions. He had a leadership style that resonated with everyone. He walked into a room and you could just see everyone lift up a bit. He was an incredibly smart man and was also a straight shooter. People like to work with winners who build groups around them and support them in crossing over the finish line without dictating to them how to do their job on a daily basis.

Matt Chapman exuded confidence but did not make people feel inferior. He motivated them to do their best. Rather than issuing commands and trying to control people, he encouraged them to think for themselves. His respect for people earned their trust and loyalty. In sharp contrast, General George S. Patton, one of America's key military leaders in World War II, guided the men under his command with a stern hand. He was tough, demanding, and a stickler for correct military behavior. But he stood tall in the first vehicle heading toward the front lines and would stride through hell with his men. He won the respect and love of those he led into battle. Two effective leaders, two vastly different styles. How would your colleagues describe your style? Does it vary, depending on the situation?

ADAPT TO THE SITUATION

An encouraging and charismatic leader like Matt Chapman knew when a situation demanded firmness; and a stern taskmaster like General Patton knew when a little honey would work better than a dose of vinegar. Pay attention to the ways effective influencers adapt to changing circumstances. Scripps Networks Interactive's Henry Ahn offered me some advice on this aspect of leadership. "You cannot be prescriptive about your approach. Development should be specific to your particular colleague's needs. And, it's most important to be empathetic."

This brings us back to walking in the shoes of those you wish to influence. If Jessica's boss senses that she is sensitive about conversations concerning her personal life, he will approach her more cautiously when he needs to talk to her about her tardiness due to a sick child at home. Also, he knows she welcomes a blunt approach regarding work. He will tell Jessica when she has taken a wrong turn with a lab experiment.

Some company cultures also favor one style over another. As Andrea Manning Weetman, a principal at Boston-based financial recruitment firm AMW Recruitment Consulting, told me during an interview, you should always ask yourself about a given corporate culture, "How can my style and demeanor best function within it?" A scientific research facility will favor a more cerebral approach than a battalion of battle-hardened soldiers.

TAKING STOCK

We're going to play a game I created called "The Influencer's Thesaurus Game." You play the role of the influencer. Below you will find a number of attributes that generally describe a highly persuasive person. For each trait, rate yourself as Strong, Mild, or Weak. Your ratings will provide some hints about modifications you may need to make in order to become a better persuader.

- *Empathetic.* Do I listen carefully to what my colleagues and friends say without rehearsing my response while they are talking?
- *Open-minded.* Do I welcome ideas and opinions that differ from my own?
- *Alluring.* Do people gravitate toward me in business and social situations?
- *Cogent.* Do people find my arguments reasonable, even if they disagree with my position on an issue?
- *Logical.* Do I take care to articulate my ideas in a clear, concise, and compelling fashion?
- *Convincing.* Do people change their minds about an issue after I offer my opinion on it?
- *Eloquent.* Do people pay attention to me when I speak?
- *Energetic.* Do I display positive body language that aligns with my conversation?
- *Inspiring.* Do people get excited when I suggest a plan of action?
- *Powerful.* Do people look up to me and come to me for advice and support?

Let's see how Jessica fared with this exercise. Trying hard to evaluate herself with complete honesty, she ranked herself as weak in four areas: *empathetic, open-minded, alluring,* and *powerful.* Her lack of social interaction with her colleagues had impaired her development of those traits. She gave herself a medium rating with respect to *energetic* and *inspiring.* Her aloofness and unwelcoming body language certainly worked against her. On the plus side, she could confidently award herself strong marks for *eloquent, cogent, logical,* and *convincing.* Her colleagues respected her scientific approach to issues, which gave her a solid base on which to build her skills in the other areas.

REMAIN FAITHFUL TO YOUR CORE VALUES

While you need to adapt your influence style to different situations, you must remain faithful to your core values. General Patton would not have gained influence over a group of pacifists with his gruff military style, but he would not have found it easy to influence them any other way, either. By the same token, a person who believes in a collaborative approach to decision making would probably make a poor platoon leader.

British transplant Colin Bodell, Executive Vice President and Chief Technology Officer at Time Inc., one of the largest media companies in the world, shared with me how he maintains his strong belief in transparency as he strives to engage and lead his staff of 1,200 people:

I believe that the best morale tool I can provide my staff with is to frequently and continually share open, honest, transparent communication. If my communication is canned and/or inauthentic, it will fall flat. Rather, I work to share my natural passions and enthusiasm about our work with everyone I can touch. While I can't talk directly to them all, I do try to connect on a personal level on our "all-staff" calls and make sure to showcase our team members who are doing extraordinary things.

You must often execute a delicate balancing act. While you need to not impose your personal values on others, you should expect others to respect your principles.

ASKING THE TOUGH QUESTIONS ABOUT
the Art of Influence

In our list of words describing people who exercise great influence, we included the word "power." Anyone who strongly influences others exerts a certain amount of power. When you influence someone to embrace your perspective, you feel powerful. These six questions should help you retain the balance of power that takes place when you are leading.

1. **How do I feel about influencing others?** Successful influencing may make you feel powerful, but it can also make you feel uncomfortable.
2. **Do I approach the people I hope to influence with confidence?** Feelings of confidence usually signal a sense that you wish to influence people for their benefit.
3. **Do I give up easily when I encounter resistance to my ideas and suggestions?** Sometimes you need to present your perspective several times before you win a convert to your point of view, but other times you need to accept the

fact that no amount of influence will bring the other person around to your way of thinking.

4. **Have I ever followed an influential person down a path that made me feel uncomfortable?** While you can often make more progress toward your goals by doing something that takes you out of your comfort zone, a high degree of discomfort may indicate that you may have abandoned your core values.

5. **Do I use my influence to help the people around me perform to the best of their abilities?** You often benefit from the best performances of other people.

6. **Would other people describe me as a stubborn person or as an open-minded colleague?** Know when to stick to your guns and when to lay them aside.

The Influence Window

Let's turn to the Influence Window©, a model we developed that will help you harness the power of collaboration and, as a result, become a more confident leader. The Influence Window helps you match your choice of leadership style to the dynamics of a particular working relationship and the urgency of the situation. You can use the subtle art of influence to keep you in the driver's seat as you wind your way through countless negotiations.

This model draws on research conducted by Patrick Curran with Keilty, Goldsmith and Boone.[1] The Influence Window displays four major ways you can exert your influence: collaborate, guide, direct, and disengage. While many situations call for a mix of styles, in most interactions you will emphasize the one best

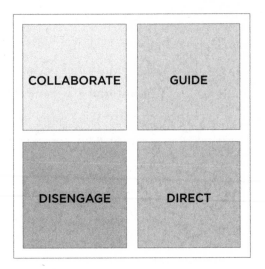

FIGURE 8-1 The Influence Window

suited to the occasion. It all depends on the urgency and complexity of the situation, as well as on the experience and competency of the people involved. Let's take a quick look at each of these approaches.

COLLABORATE TOWARD UNDERSTANDING

Collaboration gets the best results when two or more people of more or less equal competence and experience come together to achieve a goal or solve a problem. The teammates act as equals, accepting ownership for the result, exercising deep empathy, sharing candid opinions, lending loyal support, and listening carefully to different perspectives. No one acts defensively or covers up mistakes. Openness, transparency, full disclosure, and a shared sense of accountability rule all interactions.

At the lab, collaboration would work best for Jessica's team, if everyone possessed similarly advanced degrees and had worked in the field for many years. But this was not the case, so a different approach would be used.

GUIDE TOWARD RESULTS

However, some situations do not lend themselves to collaboration. In some cases, once you have decided that you have collected enough information from the other party and have formed an opinion about the matter at hand, you find it most effective to move into a guiding style. You make this shift when the situation demands a strategy or solution in a short period of time, when the people involved bring different levels of experience and competency to the undertaking.

This is when the group needs someone to guide them toward the best strategy or solution. They feel some pressure to perform quickly. A good guide uses logic, careful explanations, patience, and encouragement to move people toward desired results. People in the group must respect and remain open to learning from the guide. Note that the guide does not operate in an authoritarian "command-and-control" mode but serves as a coach, a teacher, and a model for the behavior that he expects from the group.

When Jessica joined a new team at the lab, it was composed of a few raw recruits and others with far less experience than she brings to the project. Because the new team has to meet a tight deadline, it will get the best results if she patiently coaches and teaches her new teammates at opportune moments.

DIRECT TOWARD COMPLIANCE

There comes a time when collaboration and guidance won't get the right result because you need a group with varying degrees of competence and experience to comply immediately with an order and cannot afford the time discussing the matter. You must state your case without little or no explanation and make it clear that you expect people to follow orders, no questions asked.

This approach applies to situations where you have to deal with a chronic problem, perhaps a person's unacceptable rebellion or tendency to sabotage the work of others, or an extreme emergency, such as an impending bankruptcy, where inaction can invite dire consequences.

At Jess's lab, the team has run out of time on a major initiative. The boss cannot afford for the team to debate the next step. They must pull together in one direction, and they must do it *now*. He orders them to get moving. When Walter objects, the boss says, "I know you disagree, Walt, but I need you to do what I say, and do it immediately. Otherwise all our jobs are in jeopardy."

DISENGAGE TO REFRESH YOUR MIND

When nothing you do exerts the influence needed to achieve the objective or solve the problem, you may need to disengage from the group and step back to consider your options. Do not think of this approach as surrender or rejecting accountability. Yes, you might decide that you want to leave this group or situation altogether, but, more often than not, it is helpful to use a brief period of disengagement to refresh your mind. At the end of your "vacation" from the situation, you can reengage with more energy and creativity.

Sometimes, in your absence, groups make significant progress on their own. When you return, you can use that progress as a way to stimulate yourself and the group to keep working hard. If Jessica gets stuck and starts to feel the pressure so intensely that she can barely think straight, that's the time for her to say, "Look, guys, all this stress is burning me out. I'm taking a long weekend to recharge my batteries. I'll come back in a much more positive frame of mind and we can resolve this issue then."

TAKING STOCK

When I teach people how to use the Influence Window I usually spend a full day helping them role-play each of the four basic styles. Pretend you're writing the scripts for four different episodes for a training video. In Episode 1, you must create a situation in which a collaborative approach makes the most sense. Then do the same for Episodes 2, 3, and 4, where three other situations lend themselves to each of the other three styles of influence (guide, direct, and disengage). And keep in mind, these styles are most effective when you have prioritized applying the Power Bank to your relationship first. Without an invesment in your power bank with someone, it can be very challenging to be able to make an impact with the various Influence Window styles.

Base your scripts on your own experience or on actual scenes from movies and TV shows. For example, a team working on coding a new software program would find collaboration more effective, while most military operations require firm direction. In between those two ends of the spectrum you will find activities best suited to either guidance or disengagement. How would you and the members of a team behave in each of your imagined scenarios? Completing this exercise will help you develop some "influence memory" that can come in handy when you find yourself with little time to prepare a careful approach to influencing others.

Avoiding Major Missteps

Now that we have explored four basic ways in which you can influence others, let's take a few minutes to explore how you can handle some of the common pitfalls that may erode your ability to influence others.

RESIST PARENTAL MANAGEMENT

Carmen Voil[l]equé, co-founder of Strategic Arts and Sciences and co-author of *Evolutionaries: Transformational Leadership: The Missing Link in Your Organizational Chart*, pointed out that eight out of ten executives make the mistake of treating their people like children. With all the best intentions in the world, they strive to educate and protect their people from danger. Like well-intentioned parents, managers and executives can feel compelled to hover too closely over their reports to help them avoid mistakes. As Carmen warned in our interview:

Beware of the powerful impulse to be parental in your management. As a manager, it is not your job to guard, defend, and protect. Yes, you should use your role as a manager to remove key roadblocks, but you should *not* also remove all speed bumps, slippery roads, and terrain that may call for four-wheel drive while you are at it. A little struggle can go a long way when it comes to employee leadership development. As a manager, you must support, challenge, and nurture.

Exerting parental influence can cause a lot of problems during collaboration because it creates a hierarchy that erodes equality among team members and stalls learning. Of course, it does less harm when you are guiding or directing people.

TAKE A STAND

While you might think of collaboration as the ideal approach, you do not live in a perfect world. In an imperfect world, a full democracy can do more harm than good. The group debates an issue like a jury, trying hard to reach a unanimous verdict. In a messy world where there is no one right way to get a good result and more than one solution to a difficult problem, all that discussion and debate can lead to a hung jury. Days and weeks can go by with no real progress. No matter which step of the ladder you may be on at the moment, always stand up for your ideas and perspectives. As former global marketing executive Tyrrell Schmidt explained to me, "My natural bias is to prefer that everyone comes to the same conclusion and agrees with the decision. In reality that doesn't always happen, so I have to focus on taking hard stands when it's required. This requires more of a deliberate effort given my nature, particularly when I have to stand alone against a whole group."

PLAY THE HAND YOU ARE DEALT

No matter how skillfully you influence those around you, you will encounter situations in which no amount of influence will change the hand you have been dealt. The company you want to join has put hiring on hold. You cannot go over budget, no matter how much you argue for more funding. Your customer simply cannot afford to buy what you're selling. Danielle Scelfo, Vice President of San Diego's Adaptive Biotechnologies Corporation, talked to me about the need to accept certain organizational constraints:

> All successful companies are challenging to manage internally. Budgets typically fall short or can be reduced, support such as increased head count may not be available when needed, and, like life, you have to find a way to achieve your goals with the resources you are granted. Those who can manage to persevere in the face of adversity are the most successful and highly valued employee assets to any organization.

I like to think of this as a subtle form of influence. Putting your head down, keeping your nose to the grindstone, and never grumbling about challenging constraints influence those around you to see you as a valuable partner.

Jessica lost that coveted grant to Walter. Which Jessica would her colleagues want support for the next one, the disappointed Jessica who only half-heartedly works on the current project, or the cheerful, unruffled Jessica who always throws herself enthusiastically into her work?

Becoming a Good Politician

During a seminar I was teaching for the Junior League of Palo Alto, an accomplished woman executive raised her hand and said, "I am so glad we are finally talking about how to tackle politics. I have my MBA, and I recently won a local city council seat, and not once has any business educator ever brought up this subject!" The word "politics" has earned a bad reputation, but I cannot imagine a single situation in life or on the job where politics do not come into play, whether you are trying to solve a problem with your life partner about household responsibilities or are jockeying for a major promotion at work. Let's give the word a more positive spin by equating it with influence.

MANAGE RELATIONSHIPS CAREFULLY

Dr. Lois Frankel, author of the book *Nice Girls Don't Get the Corner Office* and the President of Corporate Coaching International, explained to me that effective influencers pay attention to relationship-building. Rather than dismissing politics as a dirty, manipulative game, she advises us to think of it as a means of developing solid and supportive relationships with people who can help us reach our goals.

Jessica hates what she calls "office politics," but what she really hates is the way Walter works at pleasing their boss. She herself has done little to build strong bonds with anyone at her workplace.

FIGHT FOR YOUR CORNER

Huffington Post blogger Dr. Kathleen Kelley Reardon, author of *The Secret Handshake*, *It's All Politics*, and *Comebacks at Work*, would advise Jessica to keep fighting for advancement, no matter how much she resents a colleague's political maneuvering. Kathleen learned this lesson on her way to earning tenure at the University of Southern California's Business School in the 1970s. Every step of the way she felt like an underdog because of her gender, but she drew strength from her mentor, feminist pioneer Betty Friedan, who wrote the groundbreaking book, *The Feminine Mystique*.

In an interview, Kathleen stressed to me the importance of what she calls "fighting for your corner." By that she meant that you need to make your position clear, keep moving forward, and avoid apologies and disclaimers such as, "I hope this approach doesn't upset anyone" or "This may sound stupid, but . . ." Rather, she suggests saying something like, "Here is my view, given what I've learned so far" or "Hear me out on this one; it's an idea in progress" or "Let's look at it another way."

Pulling rather than pushing and shoving people toward your point of view will win more converts than all the combativeness and defensiveness in the world. It also strengthens each application of every style.

DETERMINE YOUR DEAL BREAKER

A few years ago, my colleague Bridget shared an interesting experience with me. At the time she was working for an engineering company in the Midwest. The youngest management candidate the company had ever employed, she found herself surrounded by men in a mostly all-male industry. Her boss gave her some rather pointed advice. "Lower your voice in meetings, do not speak your mind in social settings, take off those flashy rings, and stop telling people about that big house you are building." The men in the company never received such warnings. Not long ago I posted Bridget's story on my blog, asking people what they thought of it. I received two extremely insightful responses.

Kathy Caprino, *Forbes* and *Huffington Post* blogger, author of the book *Breakdown Breakthrough,* and the International Career Success Coach at Ellia Communications, weighed in with this assessment:

> Having to adjust everything about who you are in order to "succeed" in an organization, including your style, your personality, your voice, humor, and image, reveals that you are simply not a good fit there. If so much of who you are has to be modified in order to advance and be well thought of in this culture, then the answer is that it's time to reclaim your confidence, develop and refine your personal brand, build a large support network outside the company, and get out there in the market to assess where else you can apply your great talents, gifts, and capabilities.

Nathalie Molina Niño, a global business strategist and serial entrepreneur, offered this opinion:

> *Short term*: Start working on an exit strategy; don't rush, but also don't delay. Knowing you're on your way out will help

you survive in the interim. *Long term*: If you think you can play the game and move up the ranks without something inside you dying (think "performance"), do it. But do it for one and only one reason, to get there and change the organization. Remember each of these corrosive experiences and vow never to have another woman go through them, too. Change it from the inside. But know it's a big sacrifice, and it won't work if it sucks you in or breaks your spirit. In my experience, this strategy takes a certain kind of person. It's not for everyone.

In the short term, Bridget followed her own instincts, built excellent relationships with the men in the firm, and enjoyed a successful career at that company by tempering the advice of her boss. In the long term, she moved a more inclusive and gender-balanced company.

Jessica can stay at the lab and keep plowing forward, or she can do great work there while looking for a more compatible working environment. Sometimes you need to change yourself and work harder on building good relationships and lead more confidently.

Also, of course, you can change the game completely or strike out in a new direction.

Wrapping Up

High school and college debating teams pick an issue—say, whether or not North and South America should form a European-style American Union—and then they prepare arguments that support *both* sides of the issue. At a debate tournament, a two-person team argues both the negative and positive case. Judges award the trophy to the team that makes the most persuasive cases for each position.

It's a literal laboratory for developing empathy. Now I want you to pick a topic and pretend you need to influence a friend to see it one way on Monday and the opposite way on Tuesday. You can pick something as innocuous as ordering chocolate cake or vanilla ice cream for dessert, or you can choose something as emotionally charged as whether to vote for a conservative Republican or a progressive Democrat.

Also, try imagining how you would apply each of the styles of the Influence Window—collaborate, guide, direct, and disengage—as you deliver various presentations of the pros and cons of each side of the topic.

Those who have mastered the art of influence learn to weigh two or more different perspectives in their minds, even if they passionately believe in one over all others. Whenever you find yourself in a situation where you must persuade someone to your way of thinking, remember to use the approach that best suits the situation.

chapter nine

Fortune: Keeping an Eye on Your Finances

Sasha put 110 percent of herself into everything she did. Whether she was coaching a high school soccer game, serving on the board of her daughter's private school, or working as a recruiter for a top Chicago law firm, she relentlessly pursued perfection. Of course, this single mom's obsession eventually brought her to the brink of burnout. She grew short-tempered when the girls on the soccer team did not perform up to her exacting standards, she pressed her fellow school board members to make decisions without sufficient discussion, and she began making recruiting mistakes when she did not thoroughly investigate a candidate's references. Ironically, Sasha's intoxication with success in her personal life and at work had become her biggest weakness, threatening not only her happiness but also her career.

However, a more insidious problem lurked around the corner. She had taken on a great deal of debt in the form of a huge mortgage and payments on a new Lexus, and she was paying tuition for her two daughters to attend private school. Even so, she had never given up buying designer clothes, a weakness she had developed when she first started making serious money. With such a big financial burden weighing her down, she felt she needed to push herself harder and harder, but the harder she pushed, the further she fell behind. It was a classic case of an ADABS sufferer not keeping her eye on her finances.

I like the dual meaning of the word "fortune": the good luck you create when you take careful steps to pursue your true calling, and the finances you grow as you succeed in your chosen career. Luck favors the prepared.

I tread lightly when I talk with clients about money because it is personal and the mere mention of the word ignites strong emotions. Those feelings begin early in life. Sasha grew up in a household where the family barely survived from paycheck to paycheck. Her parents could not afford to buy Sasha new clothes, and her hand-me-down wardrobe embarrassed her at school. The fear of poverty drove her to work hard and make sure she and her daughters always looked as if they had stepped out of the pages of a fashion magazine.

Someone who comes from a wealthy background can also develop a complicated relationship with money. For example, Gil grew up in an affluent environment where his parents gave him all the latest video games and a new sports car the day he got his driver's license. As an adult he felt deeply ashamed that he has not acquired a fortune of his own, even though he keeps relying on his father to bail him out of one failed get-rich-quick scheme after another.

In this chapter, we're going to take a little of the emotional charge out of the topic by discussing money in business terms. Imagine you're running a Corporation of One and must report your profits and losses to concerned shareholders. That will help you keep your eye on your finances.

Assessing Your Return on Investment

Justin Krane CFP® of Justin Krane Financial Solutions, a Los Angeles firm that helps people plan their business and personal finances, explained to me that sometimes our money life can make us unhappy, especially if we think we are not successful because we have not built a large bank account. By the same token, we can hardly claim success in our life's work if we find ourselves mired in debt. To solve that riddle, each of us must figure out our own values with respect to money.

DETERMINE YOUR FINANCIAL VALUE SYSTEM

Commercial Director of Sage One, London-based Nick Goode has learned during twenty years in the software industry that financial success hinges on figuring out your unique relationship with money. That relationship can span a wide range of feelings, from "I won't move a muscle until I know I am going to get paid" to "I'll only work at what I love." Both can make sense. In Nick's experience, those feelings arise from a combination of our upbringing, the social or religious context in which we live, our confidence, and our beliefs about individuality versus community. Few of us really think about these factors as deeply as we should.

Nick drove home his point about the diversity of feelings concerning money with stories regarding three people he has worked with (all names fictitious). The first story involved a manager, Pete, who claimed that he trusts that his employer will do the right thing when it comes to rewarding him appropriately for his work. But, suppose that Pete and the company do not share the same definition of "the right thing." Pete worked really hard to deliver spectacular results but did not receive a megabonus because the company doesn't think that's the "right" thing to do. Goodbye trust, or Pete and his employer clearly have differing expectations around rewards and performance. The second story involved a sales leader, Ray, who obsessed about how his employer would determine his compensation and spent too much time worrying and too little time working. Nick told Ray that he should focus equally on creating value and make sure his boss understands his expectations about performance-based compensation. In the third story, a product manager, Jenny, came to Nick in tears when she couldn't make her car payments after accepting less income for the sake of her team. She had forgotten that, while money indeed isn't everything, no money is financial disaster.

Nick pointed out the basic principle underlying all three of these examples: ensure that your relationship with money matches the deal you strike with your source of income. He explained, "It's the mismatch in the deal that can create resentment, unfair reward, and beliefs that someone or something else is responsible for your bank balance. Only you are responsible for that; you work for a vendor, or you work for clients, but you must also control the reward and its mechanisms to the extent that you are comfortable."

Think of your personal balance sheet as a marriage of equals between Mr. Money-Means-This-To-Me and Ms. What I-Do-For-A-Living. If either side does not carry its full weight in the relationship, if your feelings about money and your market value in the eyes of your employer do not fully love, honor, and obey each other, the marriage will hit the rocks.

TAKING STOCK

Nick Goode shared an exercise he finds quite useful when someone's weighing the chances of landing a major salary increase at work. It helps put the marriage between your financial values and your value as a worker under a microscope.

Begin by rating your feelings about your current earnings from 1 (totally dissatisfied) to 5 (totally satisfied). If your ranking falls below 4, write down your feelings. Think hard about your emotions. Do you feel cheated? Does it make you angry that your source of income does not value you highly enough? Do you feel ashamed of yourself or jealous of others who seem more fortunate? Does your situation depress you? Has the disparity between your work and your compensation ever bothered you so much that you put forth less than your best effort?

Then, again on a scale of 1–5, rate how well you have prepared yourself to do something about the feelings you listed in the previous step. Your ranking should fall between 1 (not prepared at all) and 5 (totally prepared). If you score 3 or less, think deeply about what, specifically, you can do to shift from unready to ready. Should you meet with the source of your income to discuss your feelings? Should you start looking for another job or a business to start? As you think about taking action to close the gap between your sense of self-worth and what others will pay you for your work, try to maintain a realistic perspective. You may feel you should be making $100,000 a year as a carpet layer, when the market simply will not pay you more than $50,000 for your services. If you can't live with the smaller amount, you probably need to find another line of work.

Perform this exercise from time to time throughout your career because both partners in a marriage can and do change. As your need for more income increases, as Sasha's did, you need to make sure that the value you place on your work remains in line with what other people are willing to pay you for your effort. Otherwise, you will be setting yourself up for an unhappy union.

THINK TODAY AND TOMORROW

A well-known Aesop's Fable tells the story of the ant and the grasshopper. The ant toiled so desperately all summer to store food for the winter that she led a pretty boring life. Her friend the grasshopper played all summer, and while he enjoyed himself immensely in June and July, when winter rolled around he found himself desperately hungry and shivering in the cold while the ant relished the fruits of her labor in a nice warm den. Which are you, Ms. Ant or Mr. Grasshopper? Or are you Mrs. In-Between? Whichever work and spending habits best describe you, you need to sit down and engage in an absolutely honest conversation with yourself about the balance between enjoying today and preparing for tomorrow. All work and no play makes Ms. Ant a dull girl today; all play and no work makes Mr. Grasshopper a handsome corpse tomorrow. It pays to take some time almost every day to hold yourself accountable for continually balancing the need to live life fully and the necessity to prepare for the future as your earning and spending patterns evolve.

Portland-based creative writer and producer Rick Petry shared with me how he quickly plunged into credit card debt almost the instant he gained financial freedom in his early twenties. Having grown up in a "financially repressive" home environment, he had developed a love/hate affair with money. All he heard was, "We can't afford it! Do you think we are made of money? Money doesn't grow on trees!" He hated those admonishments. Consequently, when he finally found his own little money tree, he fell in love with spending money, although faster than he made it.

It took him ten years, with the capable and loving help of the woman he eventually married, to pull himself completely out of debt, to start living within his means, and to begin saving for the future. He met the woman of his dreams, but it took a lot more than pure luck for his career and earning power to flourish once he overcame his unrealistic feelings about money.

For Rick, it wasn't just his upbringing, but also our consumer culture. In a frank conversation with me, Rick reflected what he learned about living in a society that encourages spending. "It's a vicious circle and nobody teaches you about it. Society is too busy asking, 'What's in your wallet?'" Taking honest stock of your financial situation can prove quite challenging, but it becomes even more difficult when you live in a world that encourages you to behave like a grasshopper.

When Sasha hired a good accountant to prepare her taxes, he referred her to a bankruptcy adviser who helped her design a reward system similar to a weight-loss program that helps a person get physically fit by measuring both "calories in" and "calories out." Only if she cut spending by a certain degree and increased income by a similar degree could she reward herself with that little extra "slice of the pie" in the form of a new pair of designer shoes.

Owning Your Bottom-Line Responsibilities

Throughout this book, we have talked about taking accountability for what happens next in your life. Fate may deal you a bad hand. You may fail to land that lucrative job or account, you may not win that major promotion, or you may even find yourself out of work. That's your bad luck. But only you can turn it around. However, you must get a handle on your financial situation.

SET YOUR FAIR MARKET VALUE

In Chapter 6, we talked about your career strategy. An otherwise perfect strategy won't take you far if it does not include a sound financial component. Highly respected pay strategist and equal pay advocate Patty Tanji believes that the best plans for men and women must keep money in the foreground when they make career decisions. Leaving it out of the process can severely shortchange you and your family. Yes, follow your heart, do what you love, fan the flames of your passion, but never take your eye off the need to achieve both short- and long-term financial security. "That is why there is so much political movement around encouraging more women to work in science, technology, engineering, and math fields," she told me. "That's where the money is, and that is where our U.S. economy is headed." Patty emphasized that a $5,000 per year raise in pay bolsters this year's bank account, but if you keep investing the principal and interest over the next thirty years, that raise can add almost a quarter of a million dollars to your long-term financial security. Short term and long term: that's what strategy is all about.

You must fight for that sort of security. Patty told me an interesting story about the importance of advocating for your true market value. It involved a young woman dedicated to serving others as a social worker. Despite her ardent idealism, she turned down an offer from a potential employer because she could not possibly afford to work for that amount of money. An hour later she received a call doubling the offer. She took it. Years later, she discovered to her amazement that her starting salary was double that of her coworkers. She had wisely kept her eye on her own financial needs and made more money than those who accepted less pay. You need to advocate for the value of your work and the financial security your effort provides for your family, your team, and your organization.

ADVOCATE FOR DOLLARS AND CENTS

Nick Goode observed that a lot of people shy away from talking about money with their employer. He thinks that's a big mistake.

"After all, your job revolves around money. Never feel shy about saying, 'I need money because . . . [your valid, personal reason that aligns to your first principle]'." He went on to say, "If money genuinely does not matter to you, and you can live by that principle, well done. Most people will need to buy a house, raise or support a family, have fun; be prepared for change, to retire and give back to society. I personally don't believe that money can be insignificant to 99 percent of people."

That does not mean you can ask for more money just because you want and need it. You must *earn* it. Companies struggle to hire the right people to deliver the right results. If you're delivering or surpassing the results the company expects from you, then you deserve more money and should say so. Losing your ability to deliver results could cost the company a lot more than your raise. As Nick pointed out, it could cost them a proven moneymaker.

If you work for a company and do a good job, you probably possess more negotiating power than you realize. When you feel you truly deserve a raise, try asking for between 20 and 30 percent more than you think you will get. You just might get it.

ASKING THE TOUGH QUESTIONS ABOUT
Your Fortune

For this chapter's Tough Questions I consulted with an expert on the subject of personal finance. Alice Tang, ChFC,® brings fifteen years of experience as a financial advisor to the subject. During that time she has consolidated the most important financial concerns into four essential questions:

1. **When has money created joy for me?** Think about the first time you made a major expenditure to acquire something you strongly desired, perhaps your first new car. Did it make you as happy as you thought it would? Or, did you suffer the pang of regret many people feel after parting with a lot of money? Your answer to this question will tell you a lot about the roots of your feelings about money.

2. **When has money caused me pain and tears?** This flip side of the first question usually involves the loss of money. Have you ever risked or gambled a sum of money and ended up regretting that bet or investment? Again, your earliest experiences frequently play a major role in the way you feel about money today.

3. **What is the *value* of money for me?** Review your basic feelings when you think about money. Do your thoughts energize and excite you, worry you, or make you nervous? You will probably find yourself somewhere between "money is everything" and "money doesn't matter."

4. **How would I like to be remembered?** This question takes you back to the concept of leaving a legacy, which includes not just the love and respect you won from those who knew you well, but also the money you will leave behind for your heirs. Do you want to provide for loved ones after you're gone, or do you want to spend it all before you die? If you haven't thought about this question before, you have probably been thinking too short term about your fortune.

Thinking Your Way to Financial Success

Love it or hate it, you can't do without money. So you might as well put it to work for you. I can't offer specific financial advice because each person must design a financial plan that fulfills his or her unique needs and aspirations. But I can provide some general rules for making money work for your career success.

EMBRACE PROSPERITY THINKING

Justin Krane teaches his clients to practice prosperity thinking by aligning their beliefs, expectations, and feelings about financial matters with optimism and confidence. That helps them emphasize the love side of the love/hate relationship most people have developed with money. Since both prosperity and poverty thinking can become self-fulfilling prophecies, you might as well choose prosperous over poor.

Justin proposed an exercise for putting prosperity thinking to work in your life. Ask yourself, "If I had all of the money in the world, what would I do?" Seriously. Think about it. You win the Megabucks Lottery today. What, exactly, will you do with all that money tomorrow and five, ten, and twenty-five years from now? Most importantly, will your goals in life remain the same? If not, you may have been pursuing the wrong goals all along. Suppose you quit your job as a carpet layer and decide to pursue your real dream of owning a world-class winery. Justin advises,

> Let's say with all of the money in the world, you would buy a vineyard. That may cost you $5 million. Seems a little farfetched to reach right away, right? Why not get a taste of your

goal, something that is similar or on the path of what you want to have, be, or achieve? So in this case, instead of the vineyard, why not join a wine club and spend some money that makes you feel like you are reaching part of your goal? The key is that you have to invest your money and spend your money toward experiences and things that make you happy. When you align your values and goals with your money, you will increase your return on life.

What does this have to do with prosperity thinking? It emphasizes setting goals and taking realistic steps to achieve them, no matter how much money Lady Fortune has given you to spend. It turns prosperity (think fortune) from a far-fetched dream into a touch-it-taste-it-feel-it reality.

VISUALIZE YOUR GOOD FORTUNE

Building wealth takes courage, focus, and a belief that you can make it happen. Alice Tang explained how we begin to think about money as children. Whether your parents could afford expensive toys and clothes or constantly reminded you that the family budget would not allow them to give you all that you desire, you began to harbor strong feelings about money. Even if you took it for granted, it meant something to you. An abundance of money may have made you feel safe, secure, or proud. A scarcity might have instilled feelings of insecurity, danger, or shame. Both positive and negative emotions can motivate us to succeed financially.

Regardless of your own feelings about money, you need to decide whether it will control you or you will control it. Alice's experience with her clients has taught her that before you can take control of your emotional relationship with money, you must make a conscious effort to understand it. You can replace negative associations with positive ones. If you can visualize a financially secure future, you have a better chance of creating it than if you picture yourself living out of a shopping cart under a bridge. Visualization provides a powerful strategic tool for developing a healthy relationship with money.

SCHEDULE REGULAR FINANCIAL HEALTH CHECKUPS

If you don't measure it, you can't control it. Unless you are a financial expert like Alice, you will need help planning your finances. A good accountant or tax preparer can keep you out of trouble with the IRS and help you make sound decisions about your financial future. Work with your financial consultant, be it your spouse, parent, other family member, certified public accountant, or certified financial planner to establish a short- and long-term plan. Then schedule regular, perhaps quarterly, checkups to measure whether or not you are staying on target. You might consider working online with a financial management software program such as Mint.

Regardless of the team you assemble to help you keep an eye on your bank account, consider the financial implications of every career move you make. A setback may require a short-term adjustment, as might an unexpected windfall. A smart financial partner can keep you from making such mistakes as continuing with no-longer-accurate assumptions or by moving forward with the false assumption that a surprising stroke of financial luck will repeat itself down the road.

Keeping Happiness on Your Balance Sheet

Once you have designed a unique short- and long-term financial plan that will help you grow your idea of a fortune, you need to remind yourself of the other meaning of the word, the fortune that money can't buy. Preoccupation with the bottom line can actually keep you from gaining the love and happiness that make life worth living. How do you avoid that trap? Follow Frank Sinatra's advice and "do it your way."

Author and business strategist Carmen Voillequé of Strategic Arts and Sciences describes the advantages of following your own path:

Be unconventional. When we live a life circumscribed by the expectations of others, we lead a limited life. The greatest gift that you can give yourself is the permission to be different. Let go of your need to have everyone you love or care about understand your life choices. If you are truly going to fulfill your highest potential in your life and work, you will have to push boundaries, challenge notions of "acceptable behavior," make mistakes, and redefine the very notion of success as we know it. Meeting the expectations of those around you might feel nice, but it will also mean falling far short of your greatest capabilities and passion.

This applies to money, too. Your family and your professors and fellow MBA candidates may expect you to go to work on Wall Street and make a fortune as an investment banker, but if your heart tells you would find fulfillment writing about finance and investment, for far less money, then perhaps you should follow your heart. After Sasha takes stock of her worsening financial situation she may discover that she not only needs to change her spending habits, but she would like to apply her talent with people outside the corporate walls. It would take a lot of careful planning, but she could, over time, make a successful transition from corporate life to proprietor of her own headhunting firm.

TAKING STOCK

Here's a game you can play with your friends. Gather in a comfortable spot, take off your shoes, let down your hair, and play a quick round of "Strike It Rich." The rules are simple. Pick an activity or hobby, then imagine the ways you could make a fortune doing it. Go ahead and get a little outrageous.

Here is an example: CPA Becky loves nothing more than going to the marina on her evenings and weekends and sailing on her friends' boats, whose masts she has designed. Becky begins spending more and more of those nights and weekends creating custom masts as word of mouth about her hobby begins to spread. She begins to sells her masts and eventually extends her manufacturing capacity by incorporating as Becky's Masts and hiring a few assistants to assemble them during the workweek. Voila! A year later, she stops grinding out other people's tax reports and spends every waking moment growing her nautical business. Can you envision ways in which you might earn a second source of income pursuing another type of work?

All of us tend to work harder at a job where we can apply our passion and drive and talent. That sort of work will inspire you to bounce out of bed in the morning ready to take on the world. This does not mean that everyone should leave corporate life and follow the path of the intrepid entrepreneur. Most new businesses fail within the first five years. Find an existing company where you can do what you love and do it so well you make good money for the organization and yourself. Whichever route you take, make sure you engage in work that makes your heart sing.

Wrapping Up

This may take several hours to complete, but I'd like you to create two balance sheets, one for your monetary life and one for your inner life. Take the first sheet of paper and label it MY WORK. Draw a vertical line down the middle. Across the top label the two columns "Input" and "Output."

In the left-hand column, list the ways you make money during an average month. Enter the total monthly deposit. Do the same for the right-hand column, record your monthly expenditures. Do the two columns balance? What can you do to bring them into alignment? Do you need to earn more and spend less? Perform the same exercise for your five-year plan. How much money do you visualize yourself making in five years? How will you spend that money? What decisions must you make now to turn that vision into a reality?

Turning your attention to the second sheet of paper or worksheet, label it MY HAPPINESS. Divide it into two columns, "Joy" on the left and "Misery" on the right. In the left-hand column, list what makes you happy during an average month. Have you listed both personal and work activities? To what extent does your job fulfill you? Do you love going to work in the morning? Do you find your home life highly satisfying? What can you do to create harmony between your career and your home? Under "Misery," list the sources of unhappiness in your life. Are you unhappy at work? Do you have a satisfying relationship with your partner at home? Do you long for children? What can you do to reduce the misery you experience at work or at home? What decisions should you make now in order to increase the joy and reduce your misery you will be feeling five years from now?

We have talked a lot about the folly of trying to "have it all," and the hazards of falling victim to ADABS. You can get more out of life if you keep your eye on the bank—as you do with your Power Bank—and the fortune that you store in it.

chapter ten

Pivots: Staging Your Next Act

By age forty-two, Nick had struck it rich in the field of green energy. He was a savvy entrepreneur who had built one company and invested heavily in another. When each firm went public, he pocketed millions. Now what? For a few years, Nick flitted from project to project, hoping to find an Act II that would fulfill him as much as his terrific Act I. A consultant one day, a speaker at green-energy conferences the next, and a mentor to new high-tech entrepreneurs the day after that, he never experienced the electrifying buzz he'd felt early in his career. Should he start or bankroll another cutting-edge enterprise? He had worked for a hard-charging thirty-year-old, but to this seasoned veteran it seemed like the "same old, same old." Maybe he should do something dramatically different with his life. But he could not, for the life of him, envision that next act.

It's time for Nick to go back to square one and ask himself all the tough questions I've posed in this book. He had answered them one way twelve years ago. How will he answer them now? Some will differ little, if at all, from his earlier responses, but others may take him by surprise. At this stage of his career, Nick's not dealing with surprises and setbacks that require a few course corrections; he's facing the need to reinvent himself thoroughly enough that his Act II thrills him as much as, or perhaps more than, his Act I. For you, it may be Act III or IV, but no matter how much fulfillment you derived from your earlier journey, a time will come when you need to start fresh, even if that means deciding what to do when you retire.

Recognizing Your Pivot Points

Each time we reach the end of one episode in life's journey, we must pause and evaluate our current values, level of success, and sense of fulfillment at work and at home, as well as our motivation to remain on the same path or strike out in a new direction. In my own case, I have asked all the Tough Questions I've posed in this book a number of times in my life. Then, I thought seriously about what changes I should make today in order to ensure a better tomorrow. I have performed three major pivots so far:

- When I turned thirty and realized that no amount of success as a therapist would fully fulfill my hopes and dreams.
- When I moved 3,000 miles across the country with my fiancé and felt a burning desire to create my own business

while drawing on my previous careers in psychotherapy and sales.

- When I celebrated my fortieth birthday and decided to up-level my work by committing to an in-house role with a dynamic, fast-growing company.

In each instance, the next act built on those that preceded it, just as an engaging and suspenseful drama builds momentum from Act I through Acts II and III. Not everyone pivots as dramatically I did, but I have yet to meet someone beyond the age of thirty who has not altered course in some major way. Josie graduated with an MBA from Wharton, but rather than go into investment banking on Wall Street, she put her business training to work for a nonprofit organization that helped former prison inmates work their way back into society. My friend, agent, and co-author Michael went from editor to literary agent at age forty. And Michael's accountant, Bill, never did retire from his career as a CPA, though he did move from corporate finance to personal consulting at age sixty-five, offering pro bono assistance to elderly taxpayers when he wasn't traveling around the world with his wife.

How do you recognize a pivot point? For some of us, it occurs when we receive feedback that points us in a new direction. A couple of poor performance appraisals can send you looking for a position better suited to your talent. For others, it happens when something in your current environment or a key relationship changes. The natural aging process, a disabling injury, the death of a loved one, or the bankruptcy of an employer can force us in a new direction. For Nick, it took a crash into the wall of boredom to force a reevaluation of his career, followed by years of trying on different hats in the private sector before he finally regained his passion for business as an adjunct professor of business at a state university. Sharing all that he had learned in Act I gave him a brand new lease on life.

Two cases of successful pivots happened to friends of mine, Jessica and Frederic, whose stories offer instructive examples for us.

HEED YOUR GASP GAP

Jessica Ann Morris, Communications Strategist for her own firm, jam:pr, and a mother of four, relies on her intuition to reveal her pivot points. She discovered her knack for following her instincts in the mid-1990s when she and her Boston College sweetheart, Michael, were walking along a pier in San Francisco. Michael picked up a street performer's unicycle and began riding it around the marketplace. The sight made Jessica gasp. Her heart skipped a beat and her lungs stopped pumping air. She decided on the spot that this was the man for her, forever! Now, when she weighs life and work options, she waits for that gasp. If she feels it, she acts swiftly. If not, she waits until it arrives unbidden and points her in the right direction. She calls that pivot point in life the "Gasp Gap."

Since that moment, every time Jessica considers a solution to a problem or must choose whether or not to seize an opportunity, she waits for the Gasp Gap. Does it make my heart skip? Does it make me want to shout, "Yay!"? Now, this is not some New Age goofball woo-woo phenomenon. We all shout some version of "Yay!" when something wonderful happens. In her own words:

My work isn't my life because my life works, and the Gasp Gap tool is a critical part of it. Team, respect, love: I credit my parents and sister for instilling the importance of these core values. Now they're the foundation for my family at home, clients at work, and collaborations with fellow community servants. Business as-per-my-usual is sustained by personal and professional harmony. While it'll forever require tweaks in pitch and tone, it's the duet powering my very own musical.

Call it what you will—your gut instinct, your fate, or your luck—you should look for your own Gasp Gap as you consider making a pivot in your life or your work.

TAKING STOCK

In Chapter 1, we examined the Career Success Circle and the crucial role gut instinct plays. Here I want you to think about that mind-body-spirit, gasp-inducing feeling you get when you contemplate a complete shift in direction. It happens when your body experiences a jolt of adrenaline, you inhale a huge gulp of air, and a big smile spreads across your face. If you have ever fallen in love, you know that feeling, where the world has just shifted under your feet.

With that feeling in mind, imagine that an evil wizard has cast a spell that makes it impossible for you to do whatever you currently do for a living. You must find something else to do with yourself. What would you do? Keep thinking of alternatives until your body starts to feel at least a little Gasp Gap.

NAME YOUR VITAL VALUES

Frederic Moraillon, Vice President of Marketing for Asia Pacific and Japan at Akamai Technologies, shared a poignant story about how one of his most treasured values guided him toward career fulfillment. Born in France, Frederic spent his formative years living in France, traveling a lot to Spain, studying in England, and serving in Germany as a French officer. He eventually moved to Singapore where he found his true calling: doing business in Asia. It took a few more years of working and developing a business before he finally recognized a vital value that extended far beyond his own personality.

This epiphany came when Frederic took a job as the youngest public relations manager in a five-star hotel in Southeast Asia where his responsibilities included supervising a team of five colleagues. One day, the managing director of the hotel came charging into Frederic's office demanding to know who was responsible for an embarrassing mistake that had appeared in a prominent magazine. In that split second, Frederic faced a pivotal choice: Blame someone, or accept his responsibility as team leader and take the heat. Without flinching, he took responsibility and did what he had to do to fix the problem. Little did he know that his entire team had overheard the exchange. His reaction that day cemented lifelong friendships with everyone involved, including the angry director. Frederic likes telling this story because it illustrates how values define who you are and remain intact wherever you go and whatever you do for a living: "Living abroad, you quickly realize that your beliefs and values are actually subjective, though some turn out to be universal.

This is the beauty of it, and it still is, you need to constantly question yourself."

Just as Jessica looks for the Gasp Gap when she faces one of life's pivotal points, Frederic looks to his core values for guidance. Both came into play for Nick when settled into his Act II, designing and teaching green-energy courses in the Entrepreneurial Programs for both Stanford University and the University of California at Berkeley. This pivot recaptured the thrill he had felt earlier in his business career, and it remained true to his dedication to environmental sustainability.

ASKING THE TOUGH QUESTIONS ABOUT
Staging Your Next Act

When you reach a major pivot point you should revisit all of the Tough Questions.

1. **Do my basic motivations still hold true?** Much has occurred in your life and your work over the years, so seize this opportunity to examine what really matters to you now.
2. **Have new fears arisen in my life?** Consider whether your confidence remains high or has declined in light of new fears.
3. **Do I think like an entrepreneur?** Ask yourself if you have fallen into a rut where you feel less inclined to take risks.
4. **Have I continued to link who I am and what I do to how I relate to people?** Take time to reevaluate your Power Bank and how people perceive your character.

5. **Have I orchestrated my life while pursuing my life's work?** Weigh the amount of harmony you have created between your personal and professional life.

6. **How does my present situation compare to the future I envisioned?** Decide if you need to connect some new dots to a new future.

7. **Does my network continue to serve me well?** Consider expanding or contracting the number of communities you have joined.

8. **Do I practice effective leadership?** Determine if you have mastered the Influence Window.

9. **Have I kept an eye on my finances?** Measure your fortune in both senses of the word.

10. **Do I really need to move on to a next act?** Make sure you have reached a true pivot point and not just an unexpected detour along your chosen path.

Deciding When It's Time to Make a Change

My friend and fellow career coach Bruce Hazen of Three Questions Consulting, a career management consulting firm, devised a three-step questioning process to help his clients avoid making what he calls a "white-knuckle, bail-out-of-the-plane-and-pull-the-ripcord career move." During the fifteen years he has advised people about their careers, Bruce has found that over 25 percent of them risk making a much-too-hasty decision about their current situation. Those people may not need a parachute as much as they need to look for other, perhaps better, seats on the aircraft.

In most cases, the panicking passenger has not discussed his or her situation thoroughly with a trusted advisor. Sure, an unhappy Jill may have moaned about her lousy job or terrible boss to friends and family, but she probably did not engage in a true "Think Out Loud Laboratory" with a career consultant or someone who could objectively look at her situation. When you're feeling like calling it quits, don't jump out of a bad situation until you have thought about your situation. Before we get into Bruce's Three Questions solution to career problems, let's look at some of the classic indicators that may be telling you the time has come for you to make a decision to move on before your boss makes it for you.

You know my fondness for good questions. Take a look at Bruce Hazen's outstanding book, *Answering the Three Career Questions*. He provides an excellent guidance system for keeping your career on course:

1. When is it time to *move up* in work that you want to sustain? (Moving up means progressing, not necessarily getting a promotion.)
2. When is it time to *move out* when the work or organization or your boss is no longer a fit with who you are becoming?
3. When is it time to *adapt your style* to get more success in an organization that you like?

Bruce suggests that people look for clues that they should consider leaving their current position and look for something more attuned to their desires and talent. I paraphrase his "ten classic conditions" that often indicate time for a change[1]:

1. **Your boss does not consult with you.** Finding yourself "out of the loop" usually signals that decision makers in the organization do not value your input and think the business can get along quite well without you.

2. **Your boss scrutinizes you more closely.** Increased micromanagement and documentation of everything you do suggests that your boss does not trust you.

3. **Coworkers stop conferring with you.** A growing sense of isolation from your colleagues may be telling you that people have already begin distancing themselves from you.

4. **You receive a poor performance review.** Failing to hit your numbers or achieve your goals may indicate that you and your job do not make a good match.

5. **You find yourself constantly at odds with your boss.** Frequent arguments and disagreements mean that you and your boss will never find common ground.

6. **Organizational leaders, including your boss, talk about "transition."** Mergers and acquisitions often result in downsizing and elimination of duplicate functions, possibly yours.

7. **Leaders expect new employees to turn the organization around.** The arrival of supposed superheroes tells you that the company is suffering severe problems no one expects you to help solve.

8. **Your new boss works at another site.** Those in power may be preparing to move your job to another location without offering you a transfer.

9. **Training and development activities have disappeared.** A lack of growth potential makes it clear that you have

reached a job or career plateau as far as management is concerned.

10. **Organizational leaders behave in mysterious and inscrutable ways.** Perhaps they have seen the future and the future does not include you.

Note that these questions suggest that in most cases, employees find their bosses, not the organization itself, incompatible. Before you bail out of the company, check to see if the pilot, not the aircraft, has flown you off course.

Weighing All the Options

Pivots can occur in both your personal and professional life, and a change in either can dramatically affect the other. Job loss can cause great suffering in your family; the death of a loved one can distract you from your work or even immobilize you; divorce usually diminishes the financial security of both parties and forces one, or both, to work at more than one job to make ends meet. Retirement leaves a big hole in your life if you haven't figured out what to do with all the new time on your hands. Whatever the pivot, you can look at it as a wake-up call to think about other changes you should consider making. You might decide not to change things, but quite often you will begin to move in a new direction. Let's look at both ends of this change spectrum.

STAY AND SERVE RESOLUTELY

Certain pivotal moments in our professional lives reinforce our core values and remind us why we love doing what we do for a living. National Basketball Association referee Joe Crawford gets a new lease on life when he added teaching to his on-court skill at spotting fouls. He told me when April rolls around at the end of a season, he and his referee crew will have worked hard during some seventy-five games and head into the playoffs feeling totally exhausted. Why do I do this to myself, he wonders? Then he peers into the eyes of the younger referees, who are looking to him for guidance, and he feels that old jolt of enthusiasm for his work. He can see them wondering, "What's Joe going to talk about now?" during the pre- and post-game debriefing meetings. "I am really driven to get everyone around me to perform, and that isn't always what everyone around you wants to be doing. That's where I really serve."

Staying put also made sense for my OB-GYN, Dr. Joanna Hatfield, who works in a field where the pressure can get almost intolerable. She chose her profession, believe it or not, at the age of six, when she decided that she wanted to work in women's health when she grew up. There are times now when she thinks about making a big shift into a less stressful line of work. Then, she wakes up in the middle of the night, alarmed at the thought of not honoring her original and persistent vision of working for the betterment of women's health, and says yet again, "I *have* to do this." I have met few people who seem so fulfilled by their career, even though I know she must reexamine her core values from time to time.

What about our old friend Mr. Green Energy, Nick? When he went from entrepreneur to professor, he not only continued his lifelong commitment to environmental sustainability, he grew more passionate about it as he set about motivating others to follow in his footsteps.

MOVE SLOWLY IN A RADICALLY NEW DIRECTION

No matter how radical the change you wish to make, you must keep in mind that it begins, as all new journeys do, by placing one foot in front of the other, with the belief that over time you will arrive safely at the new destination.

Fifty-nine-year-old Peter, a dental surgeon running a successful practice on Cape Cod, had studied hard to get his medical degree and for thirty years felt content serving his patients and providing for his family. But he gradually grew weary of dentistry, and knew he must make a radical change.

Peter had always loved the arts and enjoyed the supportive environment Cape Cod provides for artists of all kinds. One day an idea struck. He could take his skill working with small dental tools themselves and become a jewelry maker. The idea thrilled him. It started as a hobby, but after a few years he sold his practice and became a successful crafter of fine jewelry. He got involved in local theatre productions and eventually became creative director for a local school for performing arts. Peter did it the right way, one step at a time. And he did it with imagination.

HARNESSING SPEED AND ADAPTABILITY

No matter how brilliantly you launch yourself into a new career, unanticipated events both good and bad will take you by surprise, causing you to grow and evolve in ways as you never expected when you began the new act. None of the people you have met in this chapter, the highly successful environmental entrepreneur Nick, public relations superstar Jessica Ann Morris, world traveler Frederic Morallion, NBA referee Joe Crawford, and OB-GYN Joanna Hatfield, could have predicted at age twenty-one where life would take them ten or twenty or thirty years later. Those transitions can apply to you.

As the years fly by, you will find that successfully navigating all the opportunities and problems that come your way hinges on your ability to react to events with agility and flexibility.

SEIZE OPPORTUNITIES WITH AGILITY

When an unexpected setback occurs, you can react one of two ways. You can ask, "Why me?" or you can wonder, "What if?" and take immediate action to turn the problem into an opportunity. Chicagoan Magnes Welsh always asks herself "What if?" That has enabled her to seize the opportunities that have come her way with supreme agility. After working for Federal Express, she took a job in public relations with Kraft Foods and earned her MBA while Director of Public Relations, a position she held for six years.

When Philip Morris acquired Kraft and eliminated her job, she nimbly pivoted into entrepreneurial mode and started Magnes Communications, her own corporate communications and social responsibility consulting practice. When she landed her first big client, Chiquita Brands, she figured the engagement would run six weeks at most, but she ended up working with the company for over twenty years. Her work with Chiquita turned her into one of the first recognized experts in corporate social responsibility, sustainability reporting, and stakeholder engagement. Her next venture will be speaking, consulting, and writing about Heart-Directed Leadership, bringing more compassion and love into the workplace.

The proper application of agility usually requires expert timing. Jump aboard the Act II Train too quickly and you may find yourself stranded at a destination you hate, wondering, "Why did I make such a hasty decision?" On the other hand, you may spend so much time pondering all the possibilities of getting to Act II that when you finally decide to climb aboard, it has already left the station. Now you sit around feeling sorry for yourself. "Why didn't I make my move sooner?"

OUTSMART YOUR EMOTIONS WITH FLEXIBILITY

There's a cozy spot between Act I and Act II—or Act II and Act III. It's called The Comfort Zone Lounge, and it's easy to fall asleep there while opportunity trains go whizzing by. Then when you do open your eyes, the thought of jumping onto one of those big, fast, noisy locomotives scares the wits out of you.

Judith E. Glaser, Chairman of the Creating WE Institute—a cadre of global thought leaders who work at the intersection of brain, brand, and energy—wrote an article for *Harvard Business Review* about the human brain getting so hooked on the need to make the right decision all the time that we easily fall into the hardwired mode where we react to change with the classic "fight, flight, appease, or freeze" response.[2] Let's call the change the A Train. It's a streamlined locomotive. It offers an opportunity to join a band of courageous and successful passengers who get the most out of their life and work. But when you first catch sight of the rumbling train, it scares you. You consider trying to stop it with your bare hands, but that will undoubtedly injure you. Why not run away? You might reach safety, but you will have left opportunity behind. If you decide to wave at the train but keep yourself at a safe distance, you will need to wait for the next train to roll along. Freeze on the tracks? Now you're road kill. Judith advises us to face our emotions, take our pulse, and listen to what our bodies and not just our heads are telling us about the next act.

It all comes down to a simple choice. Do we take charge of our emotions, or do they take charge of us? Nothing helps you take control of your emotions and ease yourself out of your comfort zone more than the ability to react to opportunity with flexibility each and every time one crosses your path.

Wrapping Up

Think about the ways we use the word "heart" to describe our feelings. "My heart wasn't in it." "I didn't have the heart to tell him the bad news." "She broke my heart." Love and anger and joy and fear all make the heart beat faster or even skip a beat. I want you to consult your heart when you think about pivots you may make in your work and your life. Perhaps you're thinking about moonlighting at a small business or earning an MBA degree on the weekends or requesting a transfer to your organization's foreign office. Do these potential pivots make your heart race or does your fear of what this shift may entail creep in and take over? The key to finding your true calling, leading with confidence, and building your own good fortune is aligning what you know to be true in your mind with what your heart longs to achieve.

When your heart and your mind are aligned, you will be able to summon the courage to move forward!

Wishing Can Make It So

When my young cousin Kaitlyn Cosenza asked me to share my thoughts on leadership, success, and work/life integration for her final high school essay, I happily agreed. After all, I was just wrapping up the proposal and interviews for this book and had been thinking about those subjects. Perhaps it's genetic, but she shares my passion to understand what it takes to achieve career success and live a fulfilled life in our complex modern world. In her case, she was preparing to head off to college, after which she planned to pursue a career in sports broadcasting, get married, and start a family. She asked me rather bluntly, "As a business leader and a very active young parent, have you and your peers struck the desired professional and personal balance in your lives that eluded your parents? What is your advice for me and your daughters on how we should approach our work and life?" Here's what I told her:

> My ultimate wishes for you, my daughters, and my readers are endless opportunities to be in communion with our world's greatest riches—the majesty of Mother Nature; the hallways of our libraries, museums, and spiritual sanctuaries; and the embrace of diverse communities.
>
> And on your way to discovering all of this fortune, my desire is that you reveal to yourself that person whom you believe in the depths of your soul you are meant to be. This relationship with yourself is of the utmost importance. If you don't know and love who you are, then you'll never fully be able to love others who want to be a part of your journey.
>
> Become your own hero, the principal leader of your self-possessed life. The easiest way to do this is to take the time to listen to *your* singular voice and not the multitude of competing ones from the clamoring crowds.
>
> Don't be afraid to achieve great things. Listen to your heart and make good on its longings. The world is waiting just for you.

Notes

CHAPTER 1

1. Simon Sinek, *Start with Why* (New York: Portfolio Trade, 2011).

2. Randy Harrington and Carmen E. Voillequé, *Evolutionaries: Transformational Leadership: The Missing Link in Your Organizational Chart* (Portland: Inkwater Press, 2011), 23.

3. Gretchen Rubin, *The Happiness Project* (New York: HarperCollins, 2009).

CHAPTER 4

1. Daniel Goleman, "What Makes a Leader?" *Harvard Business Review*, January 2004.

CHAPTER 5

1. William Oncken, Jr., and Donald L. Wass, "Management Time: Who's Got the Monkey?" *Harvard Business Review*, November 1999.

CHAPTER 6

1. Peter Drucker, *Management: Tasks, Responsibilities, Practices* (New York: HarperCollins, 1973).
3. Sun Tzu and J. H. Huang, *The Art of War* (Mishawaka, IN: Better World Books, 1993).

CHAPTER 7

1. Michael Simmons, "Here's the No. 1 Predictor of Career Success, According to Network Science" *Forbes*, January 2015.

CHAPTER 8

1. P. Hersey and K. Blanchard, *Management of Organizational Behavior: Utilizing Human Resources*, Fifth Edition (Englewood, NJ: Prentice Hall, 1988), 417.

CHAPTER 10

1. Bruce Blackstone Hazen, *Answering the Three Career Questions: Your Lifetime Career Management System* (Charleston, SC: CreateSpace Independent Publishing Platform, 2013), 139–140.
2. Judith E. Glaser, "Your Brain Is Hooked on Being Right," *Harvard Business Review*, February 2013.

Index